So Many Angels

So Many
Angels

A Family Crisis and
the Community That
Got Us Through It

Diane Stelfox Cook

SHE WRITES PRESS

Published 2019
Printed in the United States of America
ISBN: 978-1-63152-640-4 (pbk)
ISBN: 978-1-63152-641-1 (ebk)

Library of Congress Control Number: 2019938033

For information, address:
She Writes Press
1569 Solano Ave #546
Berkeley, CA 94707

She Writes Press is a division of SparkPoint Studio, LLC.

To my sons, the best boys. You inspire me.
Being your mom is the great joy of my life.
With love,
the Luckiest Mom

Never, never, never give up.

—Winston Churchill

It was quite amazing, really, how that one short phone call profoundly changed everything in our lives. In many ways it was a wonderful, ordinary Monday spring afternoon. My older son, Michael, eleven at the time, had a good buddy over at our house for a playdate after school. In no time at all, my two cherubs and the guest had mowed their way through a bag of Goldfish and several rounds of juice boxes.

Each time I looked outside to check on them, they were on the swing set or running around playing Pokémon. This was long before Pokémon Go, but the boys had their own version of this game way back then. I heard them shouting, "Pikachu or Charizard?" as I was paying bills at the kitchen table. It was warm for May, and the boys were sweaty by the time I started trying to round them up.

Billy's mom had asked me to drive him home. I walked out onto the deck and hollered, "Come on you three, time to go." It took me a few minutes to hand out pretzel rods for the ride, make sure nobody had to pee, gather up Billy's backpack and lunchbox, and pile the three boys into the car. I needed to make sure that we dropped Billy off with enough time to get home, have a bite of dinner, get my younger son, Bobby, into his Tee Ball uniform, and then drive to the field.

I felt accomplished as I pulled out of our neighborhood and onto the main road for the ten-minute drive to Billy's house. We were on time! The boys were giggling and poking each other in the back seat. Bobby was so excited about his game. This was only the second of the season for him. But the sky was getting darker, the humidity growing, and I was afraid the game would be canceled. Having to deal with a disappointed eight-year-old could make for a very long evening. I had the tunes cranked in the car and was humming along to Three Doors Down's "When I'm Gone." Then my phone rang.

The phone said BLOCKED so I had no idea who was calling me. Cell phones were common in 2003, but we were not quite as attached to them as we are now. It was unusual for me to get a call on my cell. I figured it was the game cancellation.

I answered. It was my husband calling, and I was surprised when he asked where I was.

"Driving Billy home," I said. "He was at our house playing."

"Are the kids with you?" he asked.

"Of course." I turned the radio way down and started to get into the right lane. Was he really thinking that I'd left our eight- and eleven-year-old sons at home alone while I drove the friend home? I was starting to get annoyed. Why so many strange questions?

"I need you to pull over," he demanded.

"What? Why?" Now I was really annoyed!

"Because I have to tell you something, and I don't want you to be driving when I do."

Hmm, my wheels started to turn. *Is he not coaching the base-ball game tonight? Is he having an affair?* I really had no idea why he wanted me to stop driving. He had not been acting unusual in any way, so I was totally caught off guard. I did as he asked and pulled over into the parking lot of a local business. I jumped out of the car and stood next to it, telling the boys I had to take a phone call. Inside the car, the boys laughed and talked as I heard my husband, Jed, say, "I got arrested in New Hampshire. Can you come and bail me out?"

All sorts of things began to race through my head. *New Hampshire? What the hell is he doing there?* I pictured Storyland where we had vacationed with the kids when they were little, and Waterville Valley where we had skied. Our memories of New Hampshire were running through my head. We live in Massachusetts, he works in Massachusetts, and he had a game to coach tonight.

"What were you arrested for?"

He was silent for what seemed like ages, but it was probably only seconds.

"I was arrested for soliciting a minor over the Internet. A minor male."

I thought I might throw up, and as I looked up, I got a glimpse of the kids in the car again and managed to push back the puke. I didn't want them to see me getting sick. I held on to the hood of the car to steady myself; I was dizzy. Cars went by and people were walking in and out of the store as I stood there. I felt as if I were going to collapse onto the dirty parking lot but somehow held it together because my boys were right there. I couldn't fall apart in front of them.

It was an easy decision though. As I watched the kids in the car, I quickly blurted, "I have to get Billy home, and I am not bringing our kids up to bail you out, so I guess you should call someone else."

I hung up on him.

Even though I was numb and shell-shocked, I had an immediate mission: to bring Billy home. As I was driving to his house, I was muttering to myself, *Just get the boy home.* I was not thinking clearly and felt as if I were under water. I almost blew through a red light that I totally didn't see.

We dropped Billy off, and I had a quick chat with his mom. I tried to be "normal," but I'm sure I was behaving strangely. Ten minutes after The Phone Call ended, I was back in the car with my sons, trying to figure out what to do next.

I pulled over to the side of the road, shut off the engine, and turned to face the back seat. It was muggy, and I began to sweat right away. "Boys, Dad and I had a big fight, and he's not going to come home tonight." Many friends had husbands who traveled for work, and their kids were used to their dad being away. But it was going to be very unusual for my two not to have their dad home on a weeknight. Since Jed taught and coached at the high school level, he was always home. We had never had any sort of separation before this. I told them he was staying at his mom's house while we sorted things out. I didn't like lying to them, but I thought it was the easiest way to explain his absence. There was no way I could tell them he was going to be spending the night in jail.

Back at home, both boys were upset, of course. They were uncharacteristically quiet and looked, throughout the night, like they were going to cry. In addition to my telling them that their dad was staying at Grammy's, Bobby's baseball game was canceled due to thunderstorms. I plunked them in front of a movie, a rare treat on a weeknight. Just letting them watch television signaled on some level that we were right on the edge of a huge event in our family life. But I didn't want them to know their dad had been arrested and why.

As the boys were watching television, I wandered around the house trying to process what was going on. I bounced from room to room, unable to fold laundry or sort mail as I wondered who was bailing him out. It was difficult to concentrate on anything. I kept thinking that Bobby had to do his First Communion thank-you notes, and we had lots of baseball games on the calendar. Then I was wondering what had happened to our "normal" family routine and whether it was going to return.

We had been home an hour when the ringing phone startled me. I saw the *Boston Globe* on the caller ID screen and I was stunned. I picked up the phone, said "Hello," and a reporter barked at me, "Would you like to comment on your husband's arrest?"

"No comment," I shouted into the phone and hung up quickly. *The Globe was on the phone; how strange, my husband is going to be in the newspaper.* When the phone rang again two minutes later, I jumped on it to make sure the boys didn't pick up. This time it was a local television station, and they also asked if I wanted to talk about the arrest. I was stunned that the news had traveled so quickly. How did these news outlets know? *Maybe the reporters had listened to police scanners?* I began to wonder how big this would get.

Over the course of the next few days, I would learn that over a period of several weeks, Jed had been online "talking" with someone he thought was a teenage boy. He was using a computer that belonged to the school district, apparently sending multiple emails from his classroom. Later on, I learned that the district at first thought a student was using his computer, but an investigation had determined it was Jed. The district was already planning to confront him, but he got arrested in Keene, New Hampshire, first.

After many rounds of conversation back and forth, Jed asked the boy to meet him. They agreed to meet at the YMCA in Keene, and when Jed got there, he was arrested. The "teenage boy" that Jed thought he was talking with was actually a police officer who targeted online predators. Some of the emails were sexual, but I did not know the content or the extent of the emails at that time. After I hung up on him, Jed called his mother and she bailed him out. When he was released from custody after a one-night stay in jail and a court appearance, he went to her house and stayed there. She lived about a half hour from us. Now, he would be awaiting trial, which could take up to several years.

Those two reporter's calls were the leading edge of the media explosion that was going to occur.

Marylee was the first person I told about the arrest; I knew she was home because her son was on Bobby's team. Once the game had been postponed, I called her and said, "Please come over and help me. The shit has hit the fan."

"What's wrong?" she asked. I'm sure she was thinking that the washing machine had overflowed or the refrigerator had died. I called her first because I knew she would not overreact; she was great at problem solving, and I felt sure she would be able to get right to the business of helping me cope.

"Jed was arrested and it's bad." That was all I could get out before I began to cry. She called out to her husband that she was leaving, grabbed her purse, got into her van, and headed my way, all the while talking to me and trying to understand what I was saying while I cried. She didn't hang up until she was in my driveway.

When she walked into my house, I was sitting at the kitchen table crying with a box of tissues in front of me. I was wringing a wet tissue in my hands, and as soon as I saw her, I began to cry even harder. "Jed was arrested in New Hampshire. He tried to solicit a minor male online." She looked stunned for a minute, but she stayed calm and went right to "Mom mode," helping me strategize the next steps. First we thought we should call our boss, the local principal, to say that I would not be in school the next day. We worked together at the school as teachers' aides. She made the call for me, and we both thought she would be telling him something new, but he already knew about the arrest and said I should take the rest of the week off. The superintendent of schools had been notified by the Keene, New Hampshire, Police Department, and he had in turn notified the principals of the schools in town.

I now realized that my initial attempt to keep my sons from knowing the reason why their father had been arrested was foolish. If the news had already spread this far, just a few hours after his arrest, I had no hope of shielding them. However, I was not ready to tell them yet. I stuck with the "We had a big fight" story and thought about where they could go the next day instead of school. I felt that I needed a day to sort things out and come up with a plan for what and how to tell them.

My best friend, Luisa, homeschooled her children. We called her next to see if she would take my boys the following day. She readily agreed, and I thought it would give me a day to figure out how to tell them the truth about the arrest before they heard about it from someone else. Her generosity bought me some time.

After Marylee left, I tossed and turned all night, unable to sleep. I kept thinking about who I needed to call and what I needed to do. It was hard to wrap my head around what had happened.

At about six the next morning, while the kids were still asleep, I called Jon, Bobby's godfather. We were close, and I did not want him to hear about the arrest on the news before I could tell him.

When I was pregnant with Bobby, Jed and I had talked about godparents. We decided that Jed's younger sister would be his godmother. A good friend of mine, of Greek heritage, was also pregnant then. She told me about the Greek tradition of asking someone who is not biologically related to the child to be the godparent, thus making that person a permanent part of the family. This is very different from the Catholic tradition, which usually involves selecting a relative for the role.

Jed and I talked about it and decided that Jon was the perfect choice, since we wanted him to be part of our family. My husband had taught Jon in high school, and he had stayed in touch after graduation. Jon's mom moved out of state, but he would return to Massachusetts to see friends during his college breaks and always visited with us when he was in town. Jon was thrilled when we called him from the hospital, hours after Bobby was born, and asked him to be the baby's godfather. He continued to visit us whenever he could after he graduated from college. In August, he joined us on family vacations. One year, he came to Storyland with us and another summer to the Vineyard. At Christmastime, he would always visit and help the boys assemble and try out their new toys.

I felt like I was breaking his heart when I called him with the news of the arrest; he so admired Jed as a mentor. He kept saying, "What? Wait, what happened, Di? What are you saying?" When the news finally sank in, though, he stepped up right away. He touched my heart when he said, "I'll be over tonight, and I'll help you tell the boys."

My friend Patty rang the doorbell at seven in the morning with the local paper in her hand. Jed was on the cover. She had read it, jumped in her car, and then raced to my house, still in her pajamas, to see what she could do. We were both crying as I whispered to her on the stoop, "The boys don't know yet. Can you please come back at eight fifteen when they've gone?" She hugged me and promised to return.

Luisa picked up the boys at eight, and by eight thirty, my house was full of friends who had brought food and stopped by to see what they could do. I was on the couch for most of the morning, as the girls brought me tissues and coffee. Throughout the day, my mom stopped by a total of five or six times. She had an in-law apartment in our house, so it was easy for her to pop in.

We had built the apartment for her right after Michael was born. After she sold the house I had grown up in, she rented for a while but then began to feel like she was burning money. My mom's health was stable then, but I was concerned about her and knew that as an only child, I would have sole responsibility for her when she could no longer care for herself. Jed knew how much I worried about her, and it was actually his suggestion that we build an in-law apartment so she would not have to keep paying rent. We pooled our resources and added onto our house, sharing the construction costs with her. When the builders were done, my mom had her own place, and we had a bigger house for our growing family. She moved in a few months after Michael was born. Later, I often wondered if on some level Jed knew he was going to leave and that I would need my mom nearby to help with my boys. *Was that why he suggested we build the in-law apartment?*

Each time my mom walked into my kitchen that day, she was sobbing loudly. I was very upset myself, no doubt about that, but I finally snapped at her, "If you're going to come over, stop crying! You're not helping!" I kept thinking back to my dad's death when I was twenty-one and had to take care of her, but there was no way I could take care of her now. I had to take care of my kids and me, and I couldn't have her hanging around my house in tears. But even though I was frustrated, I definitely understood her deep sadness.

My mother had experienced many difficult things in her life. Her father had died when she was just three years old. She was badly burned in a house fire when she was in high school, and her entire childhood was apparently marked with poverty. I think that after surviving cancer in her forties, and then losing my dad after twenty-four years of marriage, she was simply worn out. Learning of Jed's arrest and knowing that it was going to cause heartache for me and my kids was devastating for her.

All morning, the girls kept looking outside, and when I finally took a break from crying, I asked what they were looking at. Our street was normally quiet on a weekday and clearly something had caught everyone's eye. I got up off the couch, put down my mug of tea, and started to walk toward the front window. Everyone in the room began talking at once: "Sit down, don't come over here." "There's a dead deer and it looks awful." "You don't want to see this." I couldn't figure out why they didn't want me looking outside. *A dead deer, what the hell? I have never seen a deer anywhere near our house.* I ignored them, of course. I guess as soon as someone tells me not to look at something, I feel compelled to look! I was shocked and totally unprepared for what I saw: every local media outlet had sent a truck. No dead deer, but there were more than a dozen giant news vans parked on both sides of my usually quiet suburban street. *I can't believe all these reporters are here to talk to Jed. What is happening to my life right now?* It was as if the street had become a giant parking lot with the kind of press that local sports teams get for their championship parades.

Shortly after I looked outside, one lone reporter was brave enough to ring the doorbell and ask for me by name.

Marylee answered the door and unleashed on him. "What are you doing here? Get out! She doesn't want to talk to you."

A few minutes later, she looked outside and saw him standing on the street a few houses up with the cameraman. She went back out and yelled some more, enough that the camera guy stopped filming.

We teased her about it: "Don't mess with Marylee." It was good to have a moment that was worthy of a laugh in the midst of the sadness of the day. Still, those giant vehicles with the dishes on top stayed parked, and the reporters kept chatting in groups on the sidewalk. We thought they would never leave.

Finally, in the middle of the afternoon, an acquaintance came by to show her support, and I caught a break. Lois and I knew each other from school events and had kids the same age, but we had never hung out together as moms. Our kids didn't play together either, so I was touched that she came to the house. After putting a huge bag of groceries on the kitchen table, she joined our conversation about the media out front. Lois said, "My brother is a reporter for Channel Seven, and he's out there. Do you want me to tell them all to go?" I looked at Marylee to see what she thought about this. I thought maybe Lois was joking. Was she really this powerful?

Patty said, "The boys will be home soon. Please get rid of them right away so the kids don't see all of this."

I added, "Please, Lois, do it." She ran outside and we watched through the window as she spoke to her brother and repeated what I had told her, that Jed would not be coming back to our house after his release. He was going to his mother's house. Her brother gave his colleagues from the other vans this information, and within minutes, the drivers had started their vehicles and pulled out of our neighborhood. I was thrilled to see them leave.

The street emptied out just before Luisa dropped off my boys. I was so relieved that they didn't see all those vehicles, cameras, and reporters staked out on our street. The reporter Marylee had chased away eventually moved to the town common to film his news segment.

My boys had enjoyed their day with Luisa and her kids at a farm which hosted an event for homeschoolers. Somehow I was going to have to tell them what their father had been arrested for, and I hoped that all the news trucks didn't return.

I prayed I could shield them, but it seemed nearly impossible. This crisis reminded me of the night when I was twenty-one and was told by a surgeon that my dad might die.

Courage doesn't always roar. Sometimes courage is
the quiet voice at the end of the day saying,
"I will try again tomorrow."

—Mary Anne Radmacher, author, artist,
and professional speaker

When I was a senior in college, studying for final exams in mid-December, my mom called me to say that my dad was in the hospital. I was in the middle of typing a paper that I had only a few hours to finish if I were going to get it in on time. "Hello? Oh, hi, Mom. What's wrong?"

"Dad's in the hospital," was all she could manage to say as she cried. I must have screamed, because the girls across the hall came running into my room asking what was wrong. I was sitting on my bed shaking and sobbing. My dad was a rock who had always been perfectly healthy. He had been chopping wood in our backyard, and when mom brought him out a cup of coffee, she saw him on the ground and called 911. He was barely conscious, and she didn't know what had happened.

Later we learned that my dad had had an abdominal aneurysm that had ruptured. I was in the middle of finals, an hour and a half away at college. My mom dispatched a neighbor to come and pick me up. I walked into my living room to find several of our neighbors "sitting watch" with my mom.

The surgeon called minutes after I got there, and I spoke with him. "Your dad has a fifty-fifty chance of surviving. The surgery went well. We successfully repaired the rupture. However, in order to do that, we had to shut down all his systems while we operated. Half the patients can't recover from that. We will have to wait and see how he does over the next few days." I got off the phone and had to relay the news to my mom and the gaggle in the living room.

I was crying as I gave the report. My mom was devastated by this news, but we kept reminding each other how he had never been sick and how strong and active he was. We believed that he would be in the 50 percent group that lived. We both agreed that we would go to Intensive Care to see him first thing in the morning, as the surgeon had told me no visitors tonight. As I lay awake that night, I could hear my mom crying; neither of us got any sleep.

The first time I walked into the ICU and saw my dad hooked up to machines and wires, I fainted. When I woke up, I was in a chair next to the foot of my dad's bed and smelling ammonia. A nurse was holding smelling salts under my nose and a damp cloth to my forehead. The person lying in the hospital bed looked nothing like my dad. There were monitors and IVs, and his skin was a strange shade of yellow. My mom was holding my hand and rubbing my back, but she kept staring at my dad and crying. *How can this be happening? I should be at school taking finals and my parents should be Christmas shopping.*

The staff must have put a note in his chart because after that, every time I walked in, I would hear one nurse say to another, "Here's the daughter. Grab her a chair." It took me a few days to adjust. I never fainted after that, but I was very shaky the next few times I saw my dad. The ICU was scary; when you see all the equipment, you know that the person you came to see is in dire straits. By day five or six, I was better able to handle the situation, no longer feeling faint. But it was terrible to see my dad looking so fragile and unresponsive. He was tethered to the machines, not breathing on his own, and the future was very uncertain.

Christmas day was brutal. We drove to the hospital to visit my dad on empty roads. He was barely conscious. He definitely did not know or care that it was Christmas. Most people were enjoying the day, and we were wondering if my dad would live. For a few days after Christmas, we were given a glimmer of hope by the staff. My dad seemed to rally for a bit. When I told him that Luisa had gotten engaged, he seemed to nod. He was very fond of her. She had been my best friend since ninth grade and was practically family. He was even sent from ICU to a regular room because he'd showed some improvement. That night I went to bed thinking, *Maybe he is going make it.* I prayed so hard.

But his kidneys weren't functioning on their own, and if he survived everything else, he would need lifelong dialysis. We clung to the hope that he might actually get discharged at some point, and we tried to understand what dialysis would mean.

Our hopes for my dad's recovery were short-lived. He was transferred back to ICU just a couple of days later; then on New Year's Eve, we got the call in the middle of the night: "He is critical. Come in right away."

My dad had not regained consciousness during the last few days, but the nurses told us that we should talk to him in case he could hear us. We did that but got nothing back. "Dad, I'm here. I got a B-plus on that history paper. I heard lots of Christmas songs on the radio on the way over here." It all seemed so useless, trying to think of something that might be of interest to him *if* he could hear me.

Our priest, Father Hogan, told us that we should tell him we would be all right, that it's hard to die, and that it was okay for him to let go.

Mom and I both cried as we tried to do what the priest said we should. "Harry, it's okay, go to heaven," my mom said. I couldn't make eye contact with her as we each stood on one side of his bed trying to get out this message of comfort. Meanwhile, the machines kept pumping and bleeping, reminding us of just how sick he was. There was no feedback from my dad, no squeeze of the hand or nod of the head to let us know that he'd heard us, or even that he knew we were there sobbing all over the place. We didn't want him to die, so telling him that it was all right to go was nearly impossible. I couldn't stand to see him lying in bed unresponsive, hooked up to tubes and bags, so I tried to reassure him.

"It's okay to let go, Dad," I said. "We'll be fine, don't worry." I think it was a little bit easier for me to say this than for Mom. I kept patting his arm while she held his hand. I know that she would have preferred him to still live even if he were very sick. But I knew that he would not want to be on this earth and be sick, infirm, or in a nursing home. I was absolutely certain that my dad was going to heaven, as he had lived his whole life being kind to others. I wasn't ready for him to die, but I didn't want to see him in the hospital bed anymore.

Dad died on January 3, several days after the hospital called us in the middle of the night to say he was dying. He kept fighting and outlasted all their predictions, but in the end he finally let go.

My mother was never the same after that. She and my dad had been building their retirement home on Cape Cod, and it was half-way finished when he died. Finances were a mess and she went to work right away, temping as a dental hygienist. She also took a job as a hostess on the weekends because it was easier to work than to figure out how to fill her days without my dad. She had been diagnosed with cancer my freshman year of college; for years we had been taking care of her and handling her medical issues, and now she was in remission. We'd never imagined that my dad would suddenly get sick—even less that he wouldn't survive it.

In the summer, about six months after my dad died, I had a dream about him. It was so vivid that I still recall every detail. He was sitting on a bed in his pajamas. He appeared to be calm and relaxed and was younger than he'd been when he passed away. He looked at me and said, "I didn't know it was going to be so hard for you and your mother without me."

I don't know what I said back to him in the dream, but when I woke up, I was practically shouting at him, "Are you kidding me? It's awful without you. How could you think anything else? Mom is so sad and I don't know how to help her."

I remember thinking that he must not have had a choice about dying, even though it sounded as if he did when he spoke to me in the dream. If he had, he wouldn't have left us.

I'm an only child, and losing my dad totally changed life as I had known it. My dad, a strong and capable man, had been my rock. He had inspired me and pushed me to do my best while also always reminding me to reach out and do something kind for someone else. In the perfect world I envisioned, there would be a litany of cousins, aunts, and uncles to step in, embrace us, and console us during these two difficult events. But that world was only in my head.

Our extended family is small, and my uncle on my mom's side lived in New York. We never spent holidays with them, so my dad's passing brought no changes to that relationship. My dad's only brother had a daughter with three children. They lived nearby, and we always celebrated holidays with them. Right around the time of my dad's passing, they moved to Maine and suddenly we saw them less often. So it was essentially just Mom and me having to navigate through life. I had always wanted siblings, but I had never wished for them so desperately as I did after losing my father.

After Jed was arrested, I had the same sense of all-consuming change that I had felt when my dad died. The world was so different it seemed unrecognizable. Now I was a mom, and taking care of my two boys was my priority. My own grief and distress had to be compartmentalized somehow so I could take care of my boys.

Within a few days of the arrest, someone gave me a copy of Rabbi Kushner's book, *When Bad Things Happen to Good People*. I sat down and tried to read it one night when the boys were asleep. This book had touched my heart and helped me find my way after my dad had died more than twenty years earlier.

I read the foreword and then stopped. In Kushner's book, he says that when something awful happens, we yell up to Heaven to God and we ask, "Why me?"

God does not answer in words of course, but he sends people to help in response to our pleas.

Well then, I thought, *we are right on track, and someone is watching over us.* After the arrest we were blessed; the phone kept ringing, the mail kept coming with kind notes and letters, and the doorbell kept chiming. People brought toys, gift cards, groceries, and meals. The answering machine was full of messages asking what we needed. My college roommate and her mom brought me new clothes. Others offered the use of their vacation homes if we needed to get out of town. The kindness of friends and strangers was overwhelming, as if my husband had died. In many ways, Jed did die; our marriage certainly died, as did his teaching and coaching careers. Our family life as I had known it also died with his arrest.

Jed and I met through mutual friends when I was twenty-five. I liked him and immediately admired his career choice. I thought his commitment to education and young people spoke highly of him, and I believed I knew what kind of person he was because of his work.

Our marriage was fairly typically middle class prior to the arrest—our family had busy schedules with me working part time and him teaching and coaching. Our boys had religious education, sports, afterschool care, and playdates with their friends. We didn't make lots of money; I worked part time as a lawyer after we had Michael, and Jed was teaching at a Catholic high school. We earned enough to pay the mortgage and buy groceries, but there wasn't a lot left over for extras. Eating out was a big treat, and it was stressful if a big bill came in for a car repair or a home maintenance issue.

We had taken some fun trips before the kids were born. Paris was so memorable; we loved the wine and the outdoor cafés. As a history teacher, Jed was excited to see every historical monument and read every plaque. I teased him as I sat in the Louvre, unable to look at one more painting. "You go see as much as you want. I'm beat, and

I'm going to sit here and wait for you." My preferred vacation has to include a beach of some sort.

Jed's family had a beautiful home on Martha's Vineyard. We were able to use it one week each summer, and we looked forward to that week all year. We both loved the beach, hauling lots of sand toys, playpens, and strollers when our boys were small. Jed and I would take turns going in for a swim or reading, playing with the boys, and building sand castles. We biked each day, looking for bunnies which scampered along next to the road, Michael or Bobby in a seat on the back of Jed's bike before they were able to ride on their own. Each year we took pictures of the boys on the merry-go-round at Oak Bluffs, an iconic New England landmark.

We both loved board games and movies, and often on weekends we got together with our friends for Trivial Pursuit or Pictionary. We spent lots of time working on the house before the boys came along; I was in charge of painting projects, and he supervised all the yard work. Jed loved teaching, and I often volunteered to chaperone school dances with him to support his work. We got along well and argued rarely, usually about money. I was often frustrated with his meager salary, especially because the hours were so long during hockey season.

There was no way to know then the extent of the changes that were coming in our life. But just one day after the arrest, I felt blessed that my first fear, that we would have to move, had been quickly put to rest. People did not blame me for what Jed had done. We didn't have to leave town. Because of the Boston Archdiocese's priest scandal which the *Boston Globe* broke open in early 2002, there had been a tremendous amount of local press on the issue of sex abuse. I thought I would be judged along with him, that people would not tolerate the family of a teacher and coach charged with this crime, but fortunately this was not the case.

You gain strength, courage and confidence by every
experience in which you really stop to look fear in the face.

—Eleanor Roosevelt, US diplomat, author, and
wife of the thirty-second president

When my boys came home from their homeschooling adventure, they
didn't know that I'd been sweating their return all day. I planned to
tell them that evening about the arrest, because I needed to let them
know what had happened before they heard about it from somebody
else. Jon came to help me as did Edith, a dear friend who has a master's in social work. They both insisted on being with me to deliver
the news.

It was dinnertime by the time they got to the house after work. I
had settled the boys in on the family room rug. That was our favorite
hangout spot and the most comfortable room in the house. Both boys
were sprawled out, Gameboys nearby. I think they knew that something unusual was happening just because Jon and Edith were both
over and Dad wasn't home.

I didn't think at eight and eleven they'd even be able to grasp what the arrest meant. I took a deep breath and said, "Dad went to New Hampshire yesterday, and he was arrested for trying to do something inappropriate to a young kid." They were too young for me to be more specific than that. When I tried to say that he wasn't going to be living with us but would be moving in with his mother, I couldn't get the words out. I started to cry as I struggled with how to say it. Jon jumped in to rescue me and said that things would still be okay even if their dad didn't live with us anymore. Both boys were quiet and looked very hurt, their big blue eyes much wider than usual. They sat very still and looked at me without saying anything. I promised them that I would not ever lie to them again. I explained how much it bothered me when I had lied to them the day before when I made up the story about the argument.

I had lied about the arrest the previous day in an attempt to protect them. In many ways, though, telling the truth now freed us up. My boys knew that they could trust me to be honest with them and them with me. We didn't have it in us to lie after being so brutally victimized by Jed's betrayal.

When I was young, my parents and I lived in a very Irish Catholic neighborhood. The other families on the street had seven kids, nine kids, ten kids, and a "small" family had just three or four kids. Then there was us with only one kid. I knew from a young age that there were many benefits to being the only child. For example, my parents sent me to private school, and we had a great summer cottage. It was awkward at times in the neighborhood because I felt like I had to apologize for all the nice things we had.

But deep down, I never stopped wishing for a sibling. I was envious of the family next door with ten kids. Their house was a blast to visit—there was always a commotion and always someone to play with. At one point in my childhood, I asked my parents what would happen to me when they died. I worried about who would take care of me if I was young when they passed. I thought that this was a problem unique to me and believed that the big families would be fine if their parents died. The older kids would take care of the younger ones. I fretted so much about my family that my thoughtful parents asked our relatives and neighbors for a commitment to take me in if they died. My parents then reported back to me with a fairly long list of the many kind people who agreed to look after me. The bonus for me was that the parents of the ten kids next door were on the list. I was thrilled! I wanted to be one of the ten. Of course, I never could have anticipated one parent battling cancer and the other dying while I was still in college. When my dad passed away, the loneliness was almost unbearable at times.

Because of this, after the arrest, I was grateful whenever I watched my boys playing together that they would always have each other. From the time he first learned to sit up, Bobby's favorite activity was watching his brother. When he got a bit older, he wanted to do everything in exactly the same way as his brother did, even though there were three years between them. This manifested itself in a variety of ways, including Bobby demanding that we take the training wheels off his bike at age four so his bike could be "like Michael's." Bobby also learned to swim independently that year so he could ditch his water wings because his seven-year-old brother was no longer using them.

We had ordered a new washing machine a few weeks before the arrest, and the large, empty cardboard box had been left out on the porch. While I was on the phone thanking a neighbor for the dinner she'd brought us, the boys dragged it inside and set up a nest for themselves in the box with blankets and pillows. I kept hearing them giggling while they rearranged things inside. When I called to them, their little faces peeked out from the side of the box, and they were both clutching their favorite stuffed animals. I walked over and looked in. They looked like two puppies cuddling. Seeing them together, I was struck by the fact that they had each other. *Thank God for that*, I thought to myself. *I'm so glad that they are not only children, as I was.* "Look at this mom, we love it in here. Can we eat a snack in our box?" Michael asked.

"If we are sad, it's better in here," Bobby said.

That night, the second after the arrest, the doorbell rang after dinner. I raced to get it, worried it was a reporter, and was stunned to see our pastor and the young associate priest standing on my doorstep.

"We wanted to come and check on you and the boys," the pastor said.

I invited them in, and they sat and talked with us. My sons were altar boys and the four of us were regular churchgoers, but it was sort of shocking to see the priests sitting at our kitchen table. They asked if we needed anything. They were very kind. After a few minutes, I told the boys that they could go watch TV, and they seemed relieved to be able to walk away. I sat talking with the priests for a while. The pastor surprised me when he said, "You should take the boys and leave town for a few days." *What is he talking about?*

"Why?" I almost bit his head off with my sharp response.

He suggested that the press was going to be challenging and implied that the coverage would probably get more intense. The pastor said that, based on his experience with other events, if the press had this much material this early in the story, chances were good that they had lots more information that they hadn't released yet. I was stunned. *Holy crap*, I thought, *how will we handle more of this? Jed is the only news story these days.*

Two dear friends who owned second homes also suggested that

I take the kids and go stay at their other property, and, for a brief moment, fleeing sounded appealing. But then I thought, *How will we return? How will the kids catch up on schoolwork? How long would we stay away?*

Although it felt wrong to go against the pastor's advice, the prospect of packing up and taking off was overwhelming. I decided that we would stay in place and see what happened.

The next night the doorbell rang again, and the same two kind men were at the door. *Oh my goodness*, I thought. *We must be in rough shape if we merit two visits, two nights in a row, from two priests.* It was both touching and terrifying that they came back, and it was confirmation that we were in a real mess. The pastor asked if he could speak with me. He gestured toward the living room, and we went there so we could speak away from the kids.

"Don't play woulda/coulda/shoulda," he said.

"I don't get it. What do you mean, Father?" I asked.

He leaned forward in the armchair and said, "You married him because you loved him, and you made a life together. Don't waste your time wondering if you should not have married him. You could never have anticipated this chain of events. You don't have the extra energy to play woulda/coulda/shoulda. All your energy and effort needs to go to taking care of yourself and your boys. You have two great kids, and if you hadn't married him, you wouldn't have them, so don't ever think that your best effort at making a marriage and a family work was a failure. It isn't your fault that it failed."

I leaned back on the couch and exhaled; I didn't even realize I had been holding my breath while he spoke. As I let his words sink in a bit, I stared at all the family photos hanging on the wall: Jed and I holding Michael at his baptism, the boys on the beach building a sand castle, Christmas day opening gifts with my mom. My family had been destroyed, but he was right—I could not simultaneously beat myself up for marrying Jed while trying to make a new life for me and my kids. The pastor's kind words helped me realize that I could never wish away the marriage because I could not imagine life without my boys. I wish I could have spared them this pain, but I would never, ever wish I did not have them.

On day three, I kept the boys home from school again. Father Hogan, my good friend since high school who had officiated at our wedding, came to visit. He had called as soon as he'd heard about the arrest, and he was eager to see us and spend time with us. We took the boys to Build-A-Bear at the mall and went to the movies, his treat.

The mall was empty because it was a weekday. It was strange to be in Build-A-Bear and have the place to ourselves. It was still an appealing store with all the brightly colored bear clothes and cute accessories, but it was surreal to be there when it was so quiet. It seemed like we were on a movie set, not actually there in person, for everything felt strange and remote.

The movie theater was also missing the usual multitude of kids who were there every other time we had attended a children's matinee. The smell of the popcorn, almost overwhelming as we walked in, seemed out of place with the empty lobby and even emptier Theater #3. Usually the place was packed when we were there. Where the hell was everyone?

Oh yes, I thought, *it's a weekday. Kids should be in school. Only people who are trying to escape would hide in a theater on a school day.*

I fantasized as the movie began. It felt safe in the dark, and I wondered how long we could stay. There were no phone calls to contend with, no reporters on the doorstep. It was as if we had fallen off our usual place on the planet and landed in some new, sparsely populated world. For a little while that afternoon, I felt that we were safe, safe because of the emptiness.

Soon I realized that I was going to have to return the boys to their normal routines. We couldn't hide out in the movie theater for much longer. *How would they be received when they went back to school? Would their peers taunt them?* I was really afraid the kids might give them a hard time. Until now they had both loved their school and had lots of friends. What if that changed?

I wasn't the only person wondering about the boys going back to school. When we got back home, Bobby's second-grade teacher, whom I had nicknamed Miss Magnificent, called and asked if she could come to the house to visit. She wanted to see Bobby, to know that he was okay, and she wanted him to know that she and the other children in the class missed him. Miss Magnificent was nearing retirement, but she was still the perfect elementary school teacher. I had volunteered in her classroom a few times that year, and each time I was in awe. She seemed to smile all day, she always had the kids' attention, and she never raised her voice. The children did whatever she asked them to do. Her lessons were creative, and she was always enthusiastic. She reminded me of the stereotype of Mrs. Claus: warm, caring, with an easy laugh and a twinkle in her eye.

Bobby was looking out the window, waiting for her to pull up.

"Mom, she's here!" he yelled as he ran to the front door.

Bobby was beaming as she walked in. I offered her tea, but before I could take her order, Bobby asked if he could show her his room.

"I don't need tea, thank you. Let's go and chat in Bobby's room."

I had never hosted one of my kid's teachers in our house, so I just followed Bobby and this lovely lady up the stairs. On the one hand, it felt strange having her there, but on the other hand, I was so impressed that she wanted to be there. I was hoping she wouldn't notice the laundry baskets piled in the hallway. What an amazing moment to see her sitting on the floor of Bobby's room admiring his Lego structures and his stuffed animals. Miss Magnificent was the perfect audience while Bobby jumped around his room, holding up various treasures for her to see. Since she taught second grade, she knew all about Pokémon, Legos, and the other things that Bobby was into. She was masterful at talking to my boy about his stuff while also urging him back to school.

"Bobby, we missed you at school today. I bet Ryan would like to hear about your new Pokémon cards. You can tell him tomorrow when you come to school."

She regaled him with what his buds had done at recess and went on to tell him about the art project she had planned for the following day. I began to cry—again—because watching and listening to her, I could feel her warmth. I was amazed that Miss Magnificent put herself out there, came to our house, and was sitting on the floor of Bobby's room. *What teacher does that?* She wanted us to know that she wanted Bobby back in school. This remarkable woman went way above and beyond her job description. The boys and I recalled her visit fondly many times afterward.

Bobby would say, "Remember when Miss M. was here and I showed her my room, Mom?"

"Wasn't that so cool, sweetie? We were lucky that you and Michael both had her in second grade."

Miss M. was the first of many angels to jump in and hold us up.

The middle school principal had asked me to let her know when my oldest was ready to return to school and was surprised when I called her early the next day to say that Michael was coming back. She said to have him go to her office first so she could greet him.

The mother of his best buddy from the neighborhood was driving the carpool that day. As we waited for them on our front steps, Michael said, "Mom, I'm just going to pretend that it's a regular day."

Great strategy, I thought, hoping those middle schoolers didn't turn on him.

It was MCAS (Massachusetts' standardized test) season then, and the principal had said that Michael could take the test in her office, or even after school under test conditions. I knew he would want to take it with everybody else, though. He did and he aced it. The results came out many months later, and I wasn't surprised at how well he had done, but I was so proud of him for the courage he displayed by going right back to school and tackling the work. I think the school routine helped him cope. He was a great student, and the familiar feel of the classroom was a comfort.

On Friday, four days after the arrest, Jed called and asked me to deliver some of his clothes to his mother's house.

"Diane, can you do me a favor please? I have no clothes here. Everything is still back at the house with you. Can you bring me some shorts and T-shirts?"

He had nothing to wear since he had driven to New Hampshire in the clothes he'd worn to work on the day he was arrested. Then, after spending the night in jail, he had gone directly to his mom's. This seemed like a ridiculous request—our world was upside-down, and he was worried about what to wear? I screamed at him, "You got arrested and now you expect me to deliver your clothes? I am not driving over there. I can't look at you. Do you have any idea what you've done?"

The second I hung up with Jed, I called Maria and then Beth. "Please help me get his stuff out of here."

The girls asked when they should come. They were probably thinking the weekend, but when they heard my semi-hysterical tone of voice, they raced over and loaded *all* his clothes into their two minivans. I turned his request for a few T-shirts and pairs of shorts into a giant, rapidly executed purge. I asked the girls to empty his side of the closet and haul it to his mother's house. I had suddenly decided that I couldn't look at his stuff in our room, my room, our closet, my closet. He might have wanted shorts, but he was going to get a lot more than that.

Maria's and Beth's own kids were in school, so they needed to watch the time. They had to drop off the clothes and get back before their kids got off the school bus. When they got to Jed's mom's house, Jed and his mom were very upset to see how much stuff I had sent. They thought he would be coming back home soon and only needed a few things to wear. I knew that he wasn't ever coming back. I couldn't trust him anymore. He wanted to be with a fourteen-year-old boy, not me. I felt as if I didn't know who he was now. Sometimes I almost scared myself with the amount of rage I felt; nothing in my life had prepared me for this. At other times I was hurt and felt sorry for myself. I'd been rejected and betrayed, and I was exhausted from the constant roller coaster of changing emotions that raced through me daily, even hourly. One minute I was mad, then I was sad, then I cried for my boys, then I fantasized about a way to stay married.

My little second grader had a tough time going back to school.

The poor kid just wanted to stay home with me. The school nurse and the teacher worked hard to convince me to return Bobby to the structure of the school day as quickly as possible. They said if I let him stay home too long, I was risking a school avoidance–anxiety situation.

"Lovebug, I need you to go to school. Your teachers and your friends miss you. I'll be right here at home, and I'll pick you up if you go to the nurse and want to come home before the end of the day."

After a couple of days of being back, he got frustrated and said, "Mom, they all want me to stay at school and they don't want me to call you!"

He was savvy enough to know that the staff was working hard to keep him in school, even though he wanted to be home with me. Our amazing school nurse even tried bribing him with a Happy Meal lunch if he stayed all morning.

The mornings became a battle as he fussed and refused to get dressed. I felt terrible that we were starting each day being upset. Marylee came up with a great plan: she and her son would pick Bobby up so he wouldn't have to ride the bus. Bobby would be complaining about getting dressed and start to get grumpy when it was time to get ready for school. But then he would hear Marylee's car in the driveway, hear his friend's voice, and start to get dressed. He didn't want to be in his pajamas when his friend showed up!

What a genius she was! Seeing his buddy first thing in the morning at his house was the best motivator for my boy. For the last few weeks of school, we were able to get Bobby out the door and on his way without a struggle because he was with his friend.

When Michael had been in kindergarten six years earlier, our family and all our friends had attended Family Fun Night at the school. On a warm night in June, near the end of the school year, we brought picnics and blankets and spread out near the playground to celebrate the end of the year. I sat near Marylee and Linda, and we agreed that the night had been uneventful. When we had heard about Family Fun Night, we'd expected more, I guess. Other than the popsicles which the PTO handed out, there was nothing special going on.

"Well, we can't complain unless we are willing to volunteer," Marylee said.

"I'm in. Let's make it really fun next year," I replied.

Linda was on board as well, and the three of us recruited some other moms. Family Fun became our project. The next year we had bouncy houses, games, prizes, a DJ, popcorn, and cotton candy machines. We spent hours planning it and begging for donations from local businesses. We rented grills and served hamburgers and hotdogs, plus hundreds of slices of pizza.

The event was amazing, and we ran it that way until our youngest kids left the elementary school. My boys loved the snap bracelets and Super Balls that were given away as prizes. It was always a fun day in our house when the giant boxes of prizes showed up a few weeks before the event. Michael and Bobby loved having the "inside scoop" on the event since their mom helped to run it.

The second year we ran it, we had a total washout; it poured for hours. We had to move the event inside, and the bouncy houses were in the gym. The kids had fun, but the school was hot and sticky from the thunderstorm. In the aftermath, there was blue slush all over the hallways of the school. We were surprised that the principal let us run the event the following year after the mess it had made inside. Family Fun Night allowed me to meet many parents and families in the school as we recruited volunteers for the event. We scheduled people to work for small blocks of time so everyone could also have time to enjoy it with their kids. It seemed like everyone knew Marylee, Linda, and me because of Family Fun, even parents with children in other grades.

A couple of weeks after the arrest, Bobby's teacher invited the parents in for Portfolio Day to see the kids' work. It was an important end-of-year event and a rare opportunity to spend time with my child in his classroom. At first I didn't think that I could go. I hadn't wanted to show my face in town and had been able to stay out of public places since friends were still bringing food and groceries. I was still fearful that I would run into another parent who would say something awful. But how could I miss Portfolio Day? I couldn't let Bobby be the only kid without a parent there. *Okay, just suck it up and get over to school; you need to be in Miss M's room this morning for Bobby.*

My discomfort walking into the building didn't last long.

Miss Magnificent greeted me warmly, and I sat down at Bobby's desk to admire his work. He and I were so happy together at his desk.

"Bobby, tell me about this story that you wrote. I love the pictures that go with it." It felt good to be doing something ordinary together.

While I went through all his beautiful second-grade work, I started to breathe a little easier. For a few moments, I was a proud mom looking at my boy's work and not a mom dodging phone calls from the press about my husband's arrest. The other parents smiled or gave me half awkward waves. They were kind but they didn't get too close. I was glad of their distance. I was a proud mom enjoying my boy, not a mom consoling a crying boy who wondered if his dad was coming home. It was wonderful to have a few minutes of respite from the trauma.

As I left the school after Portfolio Day, the secretary called me into the office.

"Diane, do you have a minute? The staff pitched in and we got this for you."

She had put together a huge gift basket for the boys and me. It was filled with gift certificates to places the kids loved, like bowling and the local movie theater, plus candy and bubblegum. I could hardly lift the basket as I headed toward the front door of the building. She grabbed the door for me and asked me if it was okay that the basket had so many treats. I guess she thought maybe I was a healthy-diet-only mom. I laughed and said, "They can have anything they want these days. The rules don't apply right now." The secretary also mentioned the high school. Her colleagues in the office there were still fighting off the press. I had no idea that was still an issue there.

I loved our school and was so grateful to everyone for what they did for us.

That week, I called our pediatrician, who was a real gem. We had been going to the same one since Michael was two years old. I had a lot of respect for her and knew that she had given us excellent care over the years. I left a message with her secretary begging her to call me back ASAP. In my message I said, "I know this is unusual but my children are in crisis. Their father was arrested, and I need to ask the doctor what I should do for the boys. Please ask her to call me—this is urgent."

I hung up thinking, *This was a brilliant idea. She will have some ideas of how to take care of the boys. This is her field.* I felt a moment of calm, pleased with myself for thinking of this resource.

At the end of the workday, the doctor called me back. I asked her if she had read about Jed in the paper, and before she could even respond, I blurted out the whole story—arrested, living with his mom, kids and I devastated, and so on.

"So, doctor, what should I do for my kids?"

I was holding the phone with my shoulder, pen and notepaper at the ready so I could write down all of the wisdom I was expecting her to impart.

After a few seconds, I was frustrated by the silence on the other end of the phone.

"Doctor, are you there? What do I need to do to help my kids?"

Still nothing in my ear.

After a long pause, she finally said, "I don't know. I have never dealt with anything like this before."

Holy shit, I thought. *If she can't help me take care of my kids, who else is going to?*

Anyone can be an angel.

—Anonymous

While the press was going wild churning out stories about the arrested teacher-coach, I was concerned that the boys would be bullied or harassed at school. I was relieved when I got a call from my neighbor, whose son was Michael's best friend.

"I have good news," she said excitedly. Aaron, the meanest kid in the fifth grade, had approached her son and said, "I feel bad about what happened to Mike and his brother." Wow, what a gift hearing that was. Nobody ever gave either boy a hard time. I often wondered later if it was because Aaron was on "Team Michael." Aaron was an unlikely angel, at least at first glance, but I think beneath his rough exterior there was a sweet kid inside.

Michael and Bobby loved hearing that Dave and Marylee had given both of their boys (who were the same ages as mine) permission to take action if it was needed to protect them. The adults were worried that my kids would get hassled at school because of the press coverage. They told their boys that if anyone gave Michael or Bobby a hard time, they could punch them!

I cracked up at dinner as my boys reported this news. "Mom, guess what? DJ's mom said he can punch anybody who says anything mean to me at school." Michael was beaming as he said this.

Bobby quickly jumped in. "Andrew can too! Isn't that cool, Mom?"

The way it was relayed to me, I had no doubt that all four boys were very excited about this mission, each hoping that the protectors would be called into action. All the grown-ups were delighted that there was never a call for this eager group of defenders to be deployed.

Nick was another angel in our lives during this time. He was seventeen, and we knew him because he was friends with one of our family friends. The boys had met him at gatherings at our friend's house. Nick also dressed as the school mascot at the local high school's sporting events, so we knew him from attending those games as well.

A couple of days after the arrest, Nick called the house and said that he had been thinking about my boys and wondering how they were.

"Diane, I think the boys might not be having too much fun right now. Could I come over and bring water balloons? Maybe we can run around the yard for a while."

"Really? Water balloons, what a great idea. They would love that. Thank you so much, Nick, appreciate it." I was amazed at the thoughtfulness and kindness of Nick's gesture. I think there must have been adults who were reluctant to reach out to us because the situation was so terrible. Our story was still on the evening news and in the papers.

I was trying to shield my children from the press and felt awful that so many other parents had to have difficult conversations with their children because of Jed's arrest. A neighborhood kid asked his parents if Jed's situation was "like the priests in the news."

Some of the high school students also struggled with Jed's arrest.

A woman whose son was a student at the high school told me that a friend of his was upset about an article in the paper. Some of Jed's emails had been published in the paper, and this kid thought that he could identify himself in one of them. Jed had possibly written about the kid. Now the kid was embarrassed and in counseling as a result.

So many people suffered due to Jed's actions, yet here was Nick, a teenager, putting himself right in the middle of our upset with a giant pack of balloons. Nick had been raised by his mom, and I believe he felt a kinship with my boys. His childhood had not been easy due to his family circumstances, and I don't think his dad was in his life. A few hours after we spoke on the phone, my boys were running around the backyard, laughing and enjoying tossing water balloons at Nick. It warmed my heart to hear them yelling when they got hit with a balloon, or when they were vying for control of the hose to refill.

"Ha! Got ya!" seemed to be the quote of the day. I talked with my college roommate, Trish, on the phone, looking out the family room window and thinking that at least for that moment my boys could just be boys. Boys should be able to toss water balloons around in their backyard on a hot day. They shouldn't have to worry about media trucks.

Nick was so mature to call me and offer to give his time to entertain my kids. After that day, he was a part of our lives. He came to games and recitals, and he visited the house often.

I learned on the afternoon of the water balloon festivities that angels come in all different sizes and ages. If you are lucky, they will touch your heart. Nick's maturity and willingness to put himself out there showed him to be wise beyond his years. I was very grateful for him.

Kevin, Bobby's terrific young drum teacher, a Berklee College of Music graduate, also gave me reason to be grateful for his presence in our lives during those early months after Jed's arrest. Kevin had been giving Bobby lessons all year when the arrest occurred. Bobby and one of Patty's boys had a weekly time slot with Kevin at their house, and we got a price break since he could give two lessons back to back, without travel time in between. I came home to a voicemail message one day right after the arrest.

"Hi, this is Kevin. I can definitely do some free lessons, because I know you guys have a lot going on right now." Yet another kind person brought me to tears with a generous gift.

He didn't want Bobby to have to skip his much-loved drumming sessions if we couldn't afford to pay him.

Bobby continued with lessons for several more years, and even though Kevin had offered to teach for nothing at the end of that school year, I did still pay him. I couldn't shortchange a starving young musician. He was so good to Bobby, and I appreciated his kind offer.

The annual spring drum recital was held in Patty's living room that year with all the neighbors, grandparents, and snacks that we could pack into her house.

Bobby jammed away happily. Watching him play offered a brief respite from the turmoil that now seemed to be part of each day. Drumming was an ordinary thing, and that day it made our lives feel ordinary for a few moments too.

Our family dentist had been taking care of us since before I had the boys, and he called when he saw Jed on the news and asked what he could do.

I don't know why I suggested it, but as we were talking, I remembered that Dr. Ted was a huge baseball fan. "Would you be willing to come to some baseball games to cheer the boys on please?" As soon as I said it, I thought, *He's so busy. That was dumb. He's got his own kids' activities to attend.*

He quickly committed. "I'd love to see each boy play. What's the schedule for their teams later this month?"

In the month after the arrest, he made it to one of Michael's games and one of Bobby's games. What dentist does that? So many angels.

In the weeks after the arrest, Patty and Linda, along with a few other women, began to come over at night to sit with me. They usually put their own kids to bed and left their husbands in charge. Sometimes they came in their pajamas, and I would leave the front door open so they could tiptoe in without ringing the doorbell. I cherished the quiet few minutes in the evening just sitting and talking. If there had been a news story, we would talk about that, and they would tell me what they heard people saying about Jed. Many nights they just listened as I cried.

Ten days after the arrest, we had agreed that they would come over. It was still high trauma in our home. At nine o'clock, I heard them shutting their car doors, about to walk up the path. I was in bed, crying. The boys had gone to sleep early, and I had locked the front door. I heard Linda and Patty, and although I wanted to see them, I couldn't get out of bed to go down and let them in. I knew they were worried since some parts of their conversation drifted up to me from the front door, which was right under my bedroom.

"Should we stay and keep trying?" Patty asked.

"Let's keep calling," Linda said.

I felt I was choking on my tears. I was sobbing and could not stop.

They gave up and went home after a few minutes of knocking quietly. They had been so constant in their support, day and night. It was awful of me to leave them on my front stoop wondering where I was and if we were all okay. I should have opened the door and let them in, and I know they would have consoled me and taken care of me. But I could *not* get out of bed and go down the stairs.

I honestly didn't know if we'd ever be okay again.

Motherhood is not for wimps.

—Elizabeth Soutter Schwarzer

I think the happiest times in our marriage were when I was pregnant. We both wanted kids, and I was very fortunate. I tried to get pregnant twice in my life and was immediately successful both times.

When I was pregnant with Michael, I gained more than sixty pounds. I ate constantly and I was huge. By the end of the pregnancy, I couldn't fit into any of my shoes. Throughout the nine months, I read loads of books about pregnancy and parenting, and Jed always sat down with me when I reviewed the next month in *What to Expect When You're Expecting* so he would be prepared along with me.

I saw my doctor on my due date, and he said he would induce me the next week if I didn't have the baby by then. After a long week of waiting for something to happen, no baby came, so we went to the hospital and I was given Pitocin to induce labor at seven the next morning. By midnight, after two epidurals and still no baby in sight, things started to get scary. Jed asked the nurse why the numbers on the baby monitor suddenly changed. She took one look at the monitor and all hell broke loose. The baby's heart rate had gone way up. Within minutes the room was full of staff, and someone told Jed to pack up my stuff because we wouldn't be coming back to this room. Then I was being wheeled down the hallway. I had not actually heard anybody say, "Emergency C-section," but somehow I knew that's what was happening. I was struck by how many doctors and nurses were in the OR.

I was definitely loopy from the epidurals, fatigued and upset, but I was alert enough to be amazed by how many people were tending to me. I noticed another batch of people at my feet. I asked what they were doing. "That's the neonatal team for your baby," someone told me. I was lying flat on my back so it was difficult to look around the room to see what was going on. Also, the staff all wore gowns and masks so I couldn't really see them. I wanted to sit up, get an explanation of what was going to happen, meet everyone, and then let the surgery start. Instead, I had to keep lying flat on my back— and still—while things were plugged in and hooked up to me, all the while trying to stay calm! It bugged me that I couldn't look at the faces of the staff.

At one point I heard one staff person ask another, "Why does she keep thanking us?" I guess I kept mumbling, "Thank you" as they were working on me. I couldn't tell which of the two masked people were talking about me, but I said, "I'm just so glad that you're all here taking care of me and my baby."

Jed was not initially in the OR with me. I found out later that the staff made him wait outside until after the incision was made. Then he was allowed to come in and be near me. It was a relief when he arrived, and I felt a little less scared. *All these people are here for us?* I thought. *This is scary, but maybe we'll be okay since there are so many of them, and a whole group just waiting for my baby to arrive so they can take care of him.* I was grateful for the large staff and for their knowledge and skills. I thought that a hundred years ago, my baby and I would probably both have been casualties. Within a few minutes of getting to the OR, I couldn't see what was happening around my tummy because of a curtain, but I could hear, "Wow, look at that, oh my."

I said, "What? What's going on?" I was worried that something was wrong with my baby.

"He's huge and he has a full head of hair," my doctor said. "He's perfect."

It turned out that Michael and I both developed some sort of infection, probably due to the eighteen-hour labor. He weighed ten pounds, five and a half ounces at birth. My obstetrician told me that if I became pregnant again, he would do an ultrasound at thirty-eight weeks and induce me early if the baby was big like his brother. That way I could have a vaginal delivery. There was no way I was going to push out a ten-pound baby!

Three years later, I was pregnant with Bobby, and as promised, my doctor did the ultrasound at thirty-eight weeks and induced me the next day. He thought the baby would be around seven pounds based on the ultrasound. I had tried to eat less with my second pregnancy, but I'd still packed on lots of weight. Bobby was born two weeks before his due date after just a few hours of easy labor, and weighed eight and a half pounds. Michael was elated and referred to himself as Big Brother for months. I was thrilled to have another boy, a buddy for Michael.

Jed was very supportive during both of my pregnancies. He often let me sleep in on the weekends when I was pregnant with Bobby while he took the early shift with Michael, always our early riser. Because Jed always seemed to be a committed husband and father, his ultimate betrayal was unimaginable.

A few days after the arrest, the boys wanted to see their dad, and he wanted to see them. I felt he could not come to our town; people were upset and we were still a big news item. I thought a neutral location, somewhere nearby, might be better. We settled on a playground a few towns away from us.

Marylee told me her husband, Dave, had decided that I should not go by myself.

"Dave's worried that Jed might try to grab the kids and make a run for it. He just wants to be there in case anything goes wrong," Marylee said.

I think he was also worried about our physical safety in case Jed got violent, but he had never been violent in the past. There were just so many uncertainties that Dave wanted to meet us there. It hadn't occurred to me that I needed to worry about the visit going bad in the ways that my friends were focused on. I was more concerned about whether I would be a mess crying and wondering if the boys would be happy or upset at the end of the visit.

I was touched beyond words and grateful for the support. At that time, Dave was working lots of overtime, and I'm sure he could have stayed at work, or been home doing yard work or playing with his kids. It was so thoughtful of him to come home early and supervise our meeting with Jed so our kids would be safe.

When we pulled into the parking lot, Dave was there reading a book in his truck. He gave me a wave and continued to read while the boys played with their dad. I felt my lips quivering as I tried not to cry. The boys bounded out of my car like puppies, they were so excited.

"Hi, Dad," they both yelled.

It was a warm evening after a beautiful spring day, and the kids were happy to be outside. It was my favorite time of year, and as I felt the breeze on my face, I wondered how our lives had unraveled so quickly. A short time ago, we had been a typical family; now we were having a visit at a neutral site with a friend playing the role of security guard. *What the hell?*

Jed stood next to his car looking nervous, but there was no doubt that he was thrilled to see our kids. We said "hi" to each other, but that was the extent of our conversation. I knew that if I started talking to him, I would start yelling or crying, and although I really wanted to unload, I couldn't ruin this visit for my boys. Both had brought their baseball gloves, so they spent some time tossing the ball back and forth to Jed. The playground was empty except for us. I sat on a bench watching the game of catch while Jed seemed nervous. He kept looking over at me while he talked to the kids.

The end of the visit was tough; I didn't know when or how to end it, and we hadn't discussed it beforehand. When I announced that there were ten minutes left, both boys looked at me sadly as if to say, "Already?" but nobody voiced an objection. *I hope they get in the car willingly and don't throw a tantrum*, I thought.

"Let's go, you guys, time to go home and hit the hay." I breathed a sigh of relief when both kids gave their dad a quick hug and then got into the car with me. It was easy and I was so relieved. Jed didn't say anything to me, just nodded toward Dave and got in his car. It wasn't until the drive home that I began to sniffle, trying to hide my tears. It seemed crazy that the three of us were driving home, and Jed wasn't coming with us.

Michael said, "I wish Dad still lived with us."

In my head I agreed, but I didn't say it out loud.

"I know, bud, this is really hard," I said.

I knew my kids would suffer if we divorced, and I also didn't want the stigma associated with divorce. But each day my brain was racing—sometimes I wanted a divorce and sometimes I didn't. My whole life had changed without my having a say in the matter. I missed the family life we had all enjoyed, and I wondered if it would ever be the same again. And yet I knew, at the same time, that it would not be healthy for him to come back home to live with us.

Money was a constant worry starting right after the arrest. Less than a year before, I had been practicing law. But the company I worked for had left the state, and I was going to have to find another legal position. At the same time, Jed had gone from teaching in a Catholic school to a public school and received a significant pay raise. We decided I could work as a special education assistant in the boys' elementary school for a year while I looked for my next legal job. It was a relief to have a break from the pressures of the legal world; I could spend more time with the boys, and we wouldn't need after-school care for them since I would be working on their schedule. So at the time of the arrest, my new salary was terrible, but Jed's pay increase more than made up for it. With Jed committed to being a teacher, we knew we would never be wealthy, but we would always get by.

Many times after the arrest, I experienced a vision in my head of climbing a mountain with a boy on either side of me holding my hand. On some days, it seemed like we were climbing up in the pouring rain; at other times I was dragging the boys up or they were dragging me up. For a long time, everything felt arduous and challenging.

I had no way of knowing how and when the legal case would be resolved. There was so much uncertainty in every aspect of our lives right after the arrest. Jed was called in to a meeting with town officials about a week after his mom bailed him out. They asked for his resignation and he gave it, so he saved a bit of face by voluntarily giving up his job. He had never made a lot as a teacher and coach, but suddenly that salary was looking good compared to the minimum wage job he might be able to get.

Our very kind neighbor Gerry had his own business, a small store. He needed someone to unload trucks early in the morning and he offered it to Jed. Gerry knew that the boys and I needed Jed to have an income if we were to have any chance of staying in our home. The salary he would get was significantly less than his teaching salary, but it was something, and I was grateful for it. I had no idea how I would meet all our monthly expenses now, because even before the arrest, we never had much disposable income.

Every day, it seemed a new part of the story would appear on the news. On this day, it was the resignation. I told my boys that they could not watch television because I couldn't risk them seeing their dad on the news. As a result, they played Gameboy more, and I rented loads of movies. The boys talked on their phone to their dad, but I tried to shield them from the news stories.

Jed had taught high school social studies for more than twenty years when he was arrested. He had worked for a private school and then a Catholic school before getting a job at the public high school. In addition to teaching, he had always coached, and the new job included the position of boys' varsity hockey coach. We were thrilled with the additional income, but also proud. It seemed like he was "moving up," going from a small Catholic school to a large public school with great sports programs. Now, all this had been destroyed, and he was front-page news for all the wrong reasons.

That May was the end of my first year working in education. Two weeks after the arrest, the elementary school secretary asked me to come into the office for a meeting. Since I worked there as an aide and Bobby was a student there, I wasn't certain of the purpose of the meeting. During that meeting, the principal delivered amazing news—the district was giving me the remainder of the school year—seven weeks or so—off, with pay.

"Thank you. I don't even know what to say." I was embarrassed that my husband had caused so much turmoil in the school district where we both worked and where our kids were students. I was nervous as I sat in the principal's office. He went on to say that the town had transferred the health insurance plan from Jed to me. It seemed they were doing everything they could logistically to help. It was clear that Jed was not going to be able to return to teaching, and I worried about what kind of employment he would be able to get in the long term. I wasn't sure how I would manage to pay our mortgage.

A few days after the arrest, Bobby's good buddy was with his mom at the grocery store. She told me later that the poor kid melted down when they walked by the newspapers—Jed's mug shot was on the front page and had caught her eight-year-old's eye.

She said, "I grabbed the whole stack of papers, went to customer service, dropped the papers on the counter, and told the man behind the counter not to put them back out." She scraped her little guy off the floor and got him into the car as he cried.

Once again, I found myself feeling embarrassed by what Jed had done. My own kids were heartbroken, but the ripple effect was huge, and other children were hurt and upset too. I am certain this was just one of many tough moments that our friends and their families faced as a result of Jed's trip to New Hampshire. The story was often in the local newspaper and on TV. First it was the event itself, next the resignation from his job, and then there was a story every time he had a routine court appearance. There were many news stories during the two years that passed before the criminal case was finally resolved.

Our one reprieve from the chaos was Friday night. Movie night was a scheduled break from our busy routines. There was no homework and no cooking, so all three of us lucked out. When we started movie night, Blockbuster video was still thriving. Right after school we would drive there to consider what to rent, and sometimes selecting the movie took a while. Other times, we were able to get the latest new release and left the store feeling as though we had scored a hit.

The next decision was which pizza place we were going to order from. There were many in town. Sometimes a generous coupon would help the selection process, and sometimes we chose based on the location of the restaurant and our other errands. Walking back into the house, clutching the warm pizza box, I always felt a bit of peace. There was something wonderful about being home with no chores ahead of us for the evening. I knew we would all cuddle together on the couch under a fleece, escaping our difficult life for a little while. These evenings of snuggling with my boys are some of my warmest memories of the years I spent as a single parent. There was comfort in the routine and in the togetherness.

There was always at least one basket of clean laundry sitting on the rug—waiting for me to fold the little T-shirts or pair the endless pile of little white socks which two boys seemed to require. Baseball cleats were piled by the back door. The big window next to the couch looked out onto our backyard. The swing set and a small fort were right in the middle under a tall pine tree that shaded the yard on hot days.

At times the household tasks seemed endless and overwhelming. The boys were hungry and had homework and baseball games, even though their dad had been arrested. The dishwasher always needed filling or emptying. These tasks kept me going and forced me to put one foot in front of the other, even when I wanted to stay in bed and hide from the media.

During this time, Bobby's godfather, Jon, was a big help. Jon told me that he would come to the house one night a week to see the boys and visit with us. I don't know how he managed to fit this in with his busy work schedule, but he came weekly for several years. If it was the night of a sport practice, he would go stand on the field and cheer loudly. If we were home and it was a homework night, he would eat dinner with us and sit with the kids while they completed their assignments. He became a fixture in town, and our friends and acquaintances got to know him as he attended concerts, games, and practices. Everybody looked for him and enjoyed chatting with him. Michael and Bobby often could be heard at an event proudly telling a friend, "That's my Uncle Jon." Jed and I had definitely chosen the right person to join the family, for Jon supported us in many ways.

A few weeks after the arrest, Michael's school band had its spring concert. Jon and my mom were there, of course, in addition to Bobby and me. Jed had not been invited; he could not be near a school or children. I was so proud of Michael in his white dress shirt and black dress pants blasting away on his trombone with the rest of the middle school musicians and wannabe musicians. I was nervous being out in public, as the arrest was still very much in the news and on people's minds. I was worried that someone would give the kids a hard time or shun us because of it.

A school committee member's son and my son were in the same grade and took piano lessons from the same lady on Wednesday afternoons, and he knew me at least in passing from school events and piano recitals. I felt he had violated our privacy with an interview he had just given to the local paper, and I was furious when I saw him in the crowd outside the school after the concert.

Jon caught me giving the guy the hairy eye and gave me a "what's up" nod of the head. He didn't know who was standing behind him. I whispered to him, "That's the school committee member who talked to the newspaper about us, and I'd like to tell him to lay off."

Jon said, "I'm going over there with you," before I even told him what I had planned to do. A moment later I was standing in front of the man, and I let him have it.

"The next time you get called by the paper with a request for an interview about my family, could you think twice about it and decline? I know you love seeing yourself quoted in the paper, but my kids and I are still living in this neighborhood, and we're not going anywhere. How dare you make things more difficult for us? The press wants fodder, so could you please not give them any?"

He looked at me as if he wasn't sure who I was. I told him that our kids knew each other from piano lessons, and I saw a slight glimmer of recognition. This man was so wrapped up in himself that I don't know if he even recognized me. We had been at enough events together that he should have. He turned red, looked down at the ground, and mumbled something, perhaps an apology that I couldn't really hear. I took a breath and was about to keep on yelling at him. It felt good actually. It was the first time since the arrest that I had been able to unleash some of my anger.

But Jon grabbed my elbow and began to walk me away, reminding me about ice cream.

"Nice job, Di," he chuckled. "Remind me to call you when I need to chew somebody out."

That summer, thanks to my mom and Jed's mom splitting the hefty bill for a two-week session, both kids returned to the day camp they had always attended and loved. In previous years they attended for free since Jed was on staff there, and they had always participated for the full eight weeks. The camp staff welcomed the boys back, and they enjoyed their two weeks. They also attended the town Recreation Department's camp for a couple of weeks, a first for them. Not being at their much-loved camp all summer was hard for my boys. It seemed so harsh that they had to suffer this loss along with everything else. There was just no way that I could afford the eight-week tab.

One night in July, we met Jed and his mother for dinner. Since she had helped pay for day camp, I thought we should visit and thank her. Prior to the arrest, we had seen her often, and I had always felt that we had a good relationship.

At the end of the meal, Jed walked us to our car, and as the boys climbed in, I began to cry. I was sad that instead of coming home with us, he was going to his mother's house. I stood next to my car and said, "How can this be happening? I wish you could be home with us." I was still angry with him and didn't really want him home to stay, but at that moment I was heartbroken, and I didn't want to take the boys home by myself. I missed him playing baseball in the backyard with the boys. I missed watching TV with him at night and cuddling. I knew that the boys missed commuting to and from camp with him. And we all missed the family time going to the town beach since it was summer, our favorite season.

Jed stood next to me awkwardly, torn because his mother was standing next to his car waiting for him and was impatient to leave. I kept crying, and he didn't know quite what to do with me. Eventually I mumbled, "Go," and wiped my tears. He gave me an awkward pat on the arm and walked away. He seemed uncomfortable, and I think he felt torn. I saw her shaking her head and looking toward me strangely. She seemed annoyed. Was she angry that she'd had to wait a few minutes before she could leave?

Later I asked him what had gone on, and he said, "My mom asked why you were crying."

The fact that she wondered why I was crying spoke volumes, I think, about the dysfunction in that family. The family pattern of denial of the big issues had not been clear to me before the arrest, but it was right in my face now.

"She asked why I was crying?" I was incredulous, "Doesn't she realize what's happening here? You were arrested, we have two kids, and you don't live with us anymore." He didn't reply. She was giving him a roof over his head and a legal defense, so I guess he couldn't speak out and risk upsetting her. *What a mess! I was pissed off.*

My relationship with my mother-in-law never went back to what it had been before the arrest. She paid Jed's legal bills and supported him. He was her son, and there was no longer room for a daughter-in-law.

I fell asleep some nights wondering how I would afford a divorce lawyer; other nights I tossed and turned wondering if there was some way to hold my family together. Mostly, I was angry and felt rejected by Jed. He had clearly shown that he wasn't committed to his marriage or his family.

His sisters seemed shocked by all the events, but they were clearly in their brother's camp. The two sisters with children hosted my boys for a weekend on two different occasions in the years after the arrest. One sister lived in Delaware and one in Maryland. The third sister got divorced shortly after the arrest and also lived out of state.

The sister who lived in Maryland spoke to me on the phone a few weeks after the arrest.

"How are you and the boys doing?" she asked.

"It's tough. Our lives have been tossed in the air. They miss their dad being at home," I said.

"I'm glad I live far away and don't have to deal with it all," she had the nerve to say.

I couldn't believe it. *Did she really just say that? What the hell is the matter with this family? Why aren't they supporting us?*

I lost it and yelled, "How can you say that? You are so self-ish. How about asking what you can do to help your nephews get through this? Could you send them a card or call them once in a while to check in?" I was angry that she was happy to be far away and could distance herself from the family drama. Why didn't she want to help?

Needless to say, we didn't hear much from her after that.

I was also shocked at how little we heard from the rest of Jed's family. One of my brothers-in-law was an attorney, and I had always enjoyed chatting with him when he was in town. He and my sister-in-law were active in their church; they sang and played guitar in several different church groups. I hardly spoke to him after the arrest, and it hurt that he didn't call me. I thought we were friends, but I realized, in the end, that he must have decided to align himself with our mother-in-law, which left no room for us.

Friends and neighbors set up an account at a local bank in the months after the arrest. I guess lots of people had asked what they could do, and this was like an early GoFundMe project. My neighbor Barb stopped by one day and said, "I need to tell you something, and I hope it won't upset you." *Now what?* I wondered.

"We decided to set up an account for you at the bank on the corner, and lots of money has already been deposited. Many people have asked what they could do, and we thought this might help you and the boys."

I was blown away. "I'm not mad," I reassured her. "It's embarrassing to be so needy, but I'm very grateful. Wow!" It was touching that so many people donated, and I remember thinking that our community was extraordinarily generous. I used those funds to pay part of a mortgage payment, and then to buy the boys' back-to-school sneakers and clothes. At the ages they were, they grew out of things quickly.

Around this time, I decided that I needed to file for divorce. It was on a day when the pendulum of my wide range of emotions was swinging toward fury and away from reconciliation. I called a law school friend who practiced divorce law and briefly outlined the situation. She was low on the totem pole at her firm but promised to get back to me. Within an hour, she called and announced, "Our firm will need a retainer of ten thousand dollars."

What the hell. It might as well have been a hundred thousand. This was a huge amount, and I had no way of raising these funds on my own.

My mom immediately and very kindly agreed to loan it to me. But two days after sending the retainer, I asked the law firm to send it back. I decided that I could not handle the effort the divorce would take, nor could I handle the emotional toll of the process at that point. I didn't even tell Jed that I had considered filing. Besides, on some days, a small part of me thought maybe I could keep my family together. It was a ridiculous thought, of course. I knew the marriage was over, but I needed to hold on to the possibility of it surviving just to help me get through the day.

The group of people who thought of us, prayed for us, and helped us included people we didn't even know. Tricia had a neighbor who gave her little bottles of holy water from France. She asked Tricia to deliver some to me when we visited. I had only met the woman once or twice. How sweet she was.

One summer day, I came home to find a package on the stoop with no return address. The box was covered with tape, and the handwriting was fuzzy and hard to read. After struggling with the tape and two pairs of scissors, I finally opened the box. Inside were two very worn teddy bears that, based on their matted fur, had been much loved a long time ago. I was taken aback by these two bears, until I found the note.

"I read in the paper about what happened to you and your boys. You don't deserve it. I hope these bears cheer your boys up." The person signed only their first name and there was no return address.

I don't know who sent us this strange gift. I think perhaps that it was some elderly person without much money who hunted through her belongings to find a treasure to send to us. I thought that if so many people were thinking of us and praying for us, maybe we would come though this somehow. In return, I needed to start thinking about what we could do for others.

When I was about five years old, my parents gave me a jar and explained that I should save throughout the year so I could donate it to Globe Santa, the *Boston Globe*'s charitable toy drive. Throughout December, the *Globe* published parents' letters asking for donations from readers so they could buy toys for their kids. Sometimes my dad read the letter of the day to me, and sometimes I read it aloud at dinner. The stories were always gut-wrenching: parents needed help due to illness, unemployment, or maybe a house fire.

I tried diligently to save all year, and every December my parents would drive me into Boston so I could hand deliver my donation to the *Globe*. The newspaper set up a special office each year which was in the downtown shopping area, not at the actual newspaper offices. After I dropped off my jar of coins, we would drive around the Boston Common to look at the light display and then get in the long line at Jordan Marsh to see Santa and walk through the Enchanted Village. Doing something for someone else, coupled with a fun family outing, was a special tradition, and I looked forward to it every year. I was always excited about our Christmas trip to Boston.

My parents both taught me to think of others and to give of my time and money whenever possible. My mom still takes every opportunity she can to bake for someone who is sick or to send a card or a check to a needy individual or charity. Even at points in her life when she did not have a lot of extra funds, she found ways to give by donating her time.

As a mom, I wanted to teach my own sons about giving to others. At the end of July, a local charity was doing a "Fill a Backpack" program, and Trish and I thought it would be a good activity for our kids to take part in. Before we went to lunch and the movies, we headed to the local office supply store. The children picked out school supplies that they thought another kid would like, and we bought a couple of backpacks to fill for our donation to the cause.

"Mom, can we buy these pencils? I like this backpack." The kids ran up and down the aisles and wanted to buy everything they saw. We sipped coffee and tried to keep a running inventory of the stuff in the carriage. It made my heart glad that we could do something for someone else, and it made our situation seem a little less awful for a moment. I loved my boys' enthusiasm for the mission.

I know the way forward.

—Anonymous

In August, three months after the arrest, the boys and I were on vacation with our friends Linda and Steve and their kids at their house on Cape Cod. The trip gave us a wonderful break away from the challenges that we faced at home. Each morning, Linda and I left the kids watching cartoons on TV and went out for a walk. We did the same route each day, looking at the neighboring cottages that were for sale and admiring the beautiful blue hydrangeas that were everywhere on our route.

The first walk was uneventful, but on the second morning I had a hard time keeping up with my friend. My right foot seemed to be in my way; it caught a couple of times as we walked, and I tripped but didn't fall.

"What's wrong, Di?" Linda asked from a few steps ahead of me.

"Nothing, I'm good. Just slow today." *What's going on?* Nothing hurt, but I felt like I couldn't make my right foot do what it was supposed to do.

On the third morning we walked, I was really disappointed that the boys and I were heading home that day. Again, I struggled with our easy walk, and for most of it, Linda was several feet ahead of me, despite my efforts to catch up.

We then made one more short visit to the beach with the children, and I walked out of my right flip-flop several times. I couldn't seem to keep it on. Bobby kept helping me when I stopped to struggle with it. When he held the sandal and slid it on my foot, I still couldn't get my toes in the correct spot for the strap without help. "Why does your flip-flop keep coming off, Mommy?" Bobby asked.

"It's silly, I don't know. Thank you for helping me, sweetie."

I struggled to walk and felt very unsteady. I was sad that we had to go home; spending time with our friends at the beach had been so much fun. My right hand was also feeling strange, and I had brushed my teeth with my left hand instead of my right before we left the house that day. My right hand could not hold or grasp anything. I wasn't in any pain, but the mobility and strength in both my right hand and foot were definitely off.

Linda was worried and wanted me to go to the hospital. I was well into "tough single mom mode" and kept telling her I'd be fine. We both decided that I probably had Lyme disease, simply because it was on the news often and was associated with random, unusual symptoms. We certainly didn't think it was too serious.

I didn't want to spend any of our special, rare vacation time in the emergency room, but thankfully, Linda kept pushing me. We were outside hanging beach towels on the line to dry when she said, "Diane, you need to get this checked. Something is wrong."

"All right, I'll call my doctor and see if she can see me later this week."

"No, see if she can see you today. I'll feel better if you get looked at."

I made an appointment to see my primary care doctor on the way home from the Cape.

I probably should not have driven home since my right foot and right hand were so compromised, but we made it safely to the office.

My doctor told me to go straight to the emergency room. My mom met me in the parking lot of the doctor's office to pick up the boys and take them home. I drove to the hospital, and I was terrified. I sat in the waiting area of the ER for a few minutes before they called me in. The TV was blasting, and I was worried that the news would come on with a story about Jed. It didn't—it was a loud game show, and the even louder, fake applause from the audience was grating on my nerves. There was a little girl sitting next to me, her arm in a makeshift sling made out of a towel, and she sat on her dad's lap. "Will it hurt, Daddy?" she asked. He was very sweet to her, whispering in her ear, trying to reassure her and reading to her from a pile of dog-eared books on a nearby table. Her small pink sneakers kept going back and forth as she swung her feet. She seemed as anxious as I was.

Finally, my name was called, and I was brought in to one of the examination rooms. I wished I weren't alone, but I was also really glad that my boys were home with my mom.

I was told by a nurse that I would probably be admitted as a patient because a number of tests were needed. This was not what I wanted to hear when I needed to be home with my kids. My primary care doctor had called the hospital and informed them of my exam in her office. I was fighting back tears when the neurologist came in to see me. *She looks too young to be a neurologist*, I thought.

She was friendly and warm as she sat on the bed next to me and explained that a CT scan and then an MRI (Magnetic Resonance Imaging) would be needed to find out what was going on with me. She also confirmed that I would be admitted to the hospital.

The CT was first. I had never had one, and it was scary being pushed around on a gurney on the way to the test, watching the ceiling tiles whiz by. When the CT came back negative, the neurologist came back to tell me the good news and said the MRI would be done next. I dreaded calling my mom and my sons to tell them that I had to stay overnight at the hospital. All of us cried as my mom passed the phone around so everyone could talk to me.

After talking to my family, I called Trish to let her know where I was. She showed up two hours later with an overnight bag and announced that she was spending the night with me so I wouldn't be alone. What a gift!

At that time, her girls were young. She must have called her mom to watch the girls and told her husband to get pizza on the way home. I was grateful for all the logistics that freed her up that she could be with me.

When the staff came to take me for the MRI test, Trish stood up and planned to follow along. The tech said, "You have to wait here. There isn't enough room for you." I felt my stomach drop because I wanted her to be with me. I did not want to go alone.

She announced that she had come a long way to be with me and wasn't going to leave. She followed the stretcher as they wheeled me to the MRI center. When we got there, she was again told to wait, this time in the MRI waiting room, but again she made it clear that she was coming in. "Look, can't I just sit in the room? I don't want to leave my friend," she pleaded. The technician looked annoyed but relented, found a chair, and dragged it into the room with the MRI machine, and Trish took it over.

The technician recommended that I cover my eyes with a facecloth. "It's small in there and you don't want to see it. It might make you feel claustrophobic." I gladly took the facecloth, covered my eyes, and got through it. MRIs are noisy and can be upsetting due to the tight space. It was so much better knowing that Tricia was steps away from me while I was in the tube. Without being rude or difficult, she let it be known to the staff that she was my roommate and she wasn't leaving my side. I could hear her throughout the process, shouting encouragement. I think if they allowed it, she would have crawled into the MRI tube with me. The staff accommodated her all the way. Lucky me.

The next morning, the neurologist came into my room and said she had some news. Her expression was very serious; the fear that I had felt since leaving Cape Cod was growing by the minute. My heart was racing and I wished again that I were home with my boys.

"There was a lesion which was visible on the MRI," she said gently. "I think that you probably have multiple sclerosis." She went on to say that there was one more test she wanted to do that could positively confirm that I did in fact have MS. She needed to do a spinal tap. The fluid would be sent to the Mayo Clinic and analyzed there. I felt like the room was suddenly spinning. *What the hell was going to happen now?*

A few hours later, I was lying in my hospital bed wishing I were at home when a very cheerful nurse barged into my room and announced that it was time for the spinal tap. The neurologist came in next and she had a student with her who needed to learn how to do a spinal tap. Would I agree to let him do mine? "Of course, let's just get it done," I said. I thought it would be a relief to have it over with. The sooner we started, the sooner I would be done.

The nurse told me to lie on my side and bend so my forehead touched my knees, which was not easy. My back had to be bent to make the spine accessible so the needle could go into my spine and extract the sample of fluid. There were many voices around me. The neurologist was explaining the steps to her student. The two nurses were chatting and laughing about a TV show that they had seen the night before. I couldn't see anything except my knees. The hospital sheets smelled weird, and after only a few minutes of being bent over, I felt dizzy and nauseous. When I thought I was in the right position, the staff told me that I had to bend much further. I couldn't get into the position that they wanted, so they said, "We can move you." A few hands were then on my body, the nurses' I guess. They bent me even further until I thought my neck would snap. I made a stupid joke about trying out for Cirque du Soleil as a contortionist. One of the nurses cracked up and said I was a good sport.

I thought I felt the needle jabbing into me a couple of different times, although supposedly they had numbed the area.

"Are we done yet, guys?" I yelled since my face was in my knees and I was afraid they wouldn't hear me. I was frightened and felt very vulnerable.

"I can't stay like this much longer," I said. "I'm starting to freak out."

"Let her sit up," the neurologist said. "We didn't get it." She then patted my arm. The student was standing there looking at the floor. Nobody wanted to throw him under the bus, but clearly his first spinal hadn't gone well. I understood without anybody saying anything that he had screwed up. *Minutes of pain from the huge needle plus being bent over in half, and they aren't done? It hurt like hell and they don't have the damned fluid?*

"Diane, we'll come back in the morning and try again. Rest for tonight," my neurologist said. *Great,* I thought, *another whole night to stew over it.* I think because I was dizzy and fighting back tears, the doctor thought I needed a break before another attempt.

Then Karen came in. She was an amazing nurse from our town who was starting her shift at the hospital. She came over to my bed, grabbed my arm, and said, "Let's do it now, Di. I'm here, I'll get you through it. You don't want to wait another whole day."

She was so confident, and I really did want to get it done. After some discussion, we agreed that they would try again. The neurologist said she would do the next one. I was glad she offered, because I didn't want to give the student another chance to work on me. I needed the master. One of the original nurses stepped out to take care of somebody else, and Karen came over to hold me in position. While the medical student watched, my neurologist got the fluid. The second time around was blissfully quick. As the many medical professionals worked on me, I kept thinking, *All this is Jed's fault—he's ruined me. He's taken our family life, my boys' innocence, and now my health.* I believed that the horrific stress of the arrest and all the ripple effects of it had caused my body to shut down.

My neurologist had explained that multiple sclerosis is a neurological disease which affects the brain and the spinal cord. An MRI is used to look at the brain and the spine of MS patients to track the presence or hopefully absence of lesions. Lesions appear as cloudy images on the film, and neurologists rely on MRI scans to determine if a patient's MS medication is working and keeping the MS under control. After she relayed all this, I asked her if she could treat me once

I was discharged, and she kindly agreed to take me on as a patient. I felt comfortable talking with her, and after the double spinal tap episode, I felt that we had connected. I wanted to stay with her.

"We can treat this," she told me. She was direct, professional, and compassionate all at the same time. I clung to her words and believed that, with her treating me, I could handle it. As I sat in the hospital bed trying to grasp everything, my sweaty hands twisting the edge of the sheet, the doctor said just before she left the room, "Stay off the Internet! You'll freak out reading everything on there about MS. This disease is different in every person, and lots of things might never happen to you." I listened to her. I decided that I had enough to do to get the kids ready to go back to school without becoming an MS researcher. Another angel, my neurologist.

My primary care doctor came to visit me in the hospital, shortly after the spinal tap, and Jed came to see me at the same time. She looked at him, gave him a withering stare, and then looked back to me and said, "You know, MS is often brought on by stress."

I didn't know that, and Jed was pissed off. For weeks afterward, whenever we talked on the phone, he would say, "I can't believe Dr. T. said that." It was another example of his not owning up to what he had done. He would take no responsibility for the stress he had caused me. Throughout the summer, we continued to talk on the phone, especially at night when the boys were asleep. I would sometimes feel sad and cry and tell him I missed him. Other times I yelled at Jed and reminded him of the many ways he had ruined our family. Looking back on it now, I realize it was not wise to talk to him so often, but I was still attached to him somehow despite his betrayal. I felt he should listen as often as I wanted to yell at him.

The doctor had explained to me that the treatment for a new lesion that is causing disability is five days of intravenous steroids, which I would receive as an outpatient at the hospital. I had my first dose while I was still an inpatient.

"Diane, I don't want to wait for the Mayo Clinic results to come back to treat you. I'm confident that you have MS, so I'd like to start treating you right away."

When I got the first dose, I fainted when they tried to put the needle in for the IV. Ever since my dad was in the ICU so many years earlier, I had become very squeamish as a patient. Having blood drawn or watching needles go in usually meant that someone had to pull me off the floor after I'd passed out.

The infusion center nurses decided that it would be better to leave the port in and wrap it up so I wouldn't have to be re-stuck the next few days. I felt like I'd caught a huge break. As long as I kept it dry, I could avoid the hassle of a new needle when I went to the infusion center for the remaining doses of the steroid.

Later that night, I looked up from my hospital bed and was surprised to see the pastor and young associate priest standing in the doorway of my room. I looked at them and I began to laugh and said, "Oh no, things must be pretty bad if you are here again. We just did this in the spring."

The pastor replied, "It's good to see you haven't lost your sense of humor."

I thought, just as I had thought when they'd shown up back in May, *Doesn't someone else in the parish need them right now?* Although

I didn't want to be in such rough shape that I needed two priests, I was so grateful for their calming presence. They didn't stay long in my hospital room. They looked uncomfortable, and I felt awkward in bed wearing a johnny. They said, "Take care. We will keep praying for you and the boys." I was happy to have their prayers and support.

One of the nurses came in to check my vitals. We chatted while she worked, and she told me that the staff was a bit taken aback when they saw the two priests come into my room.

"Everyone was worried about you. We figured you must be in a bad way if you have two priests visiting!" I explained a little about what had happened back in May.

This lovely nurse told me that I was lucky to have received the diagnosis of multiple sclerosis.

"Why lucky?" I asked. It sure didn't sound good to me.

"When you came into the hospital, we thought you either had suffered a stroke, had a brain tumor, or multiple sclerosis. The first two things probably would have killed you. The MS we can treat," she responded.

Okay, I thought, *then I love MS.*

Life is an attitude. Have a good one.

—Eric Lungaard

I did not have much time to dwell on what this new diagnosis was going to require of me.

My focus was taking care of my boys, and I needed them to be confident of my constant presence. Their dad was gone, and I knew they were worried that I was going to leave too. While I was in the hospital, they both kept calling me to ask when I would be home. Every time the phone rang, I got upset. I knew that no matter which boy got on the phone first, the first thing he was going to ask was when I was coming home, and I didn't know. I wanted to be home, and I knew they wanted me there.

After four nights in the hospital, I was discharged. The boys were at day camp since it was a Tuesday, so my mom was by herself when she picked me up. I was thrilled to be in her car and wearing my own clothes. We got some groceries, and before long I was on the couch in my family room, waiting for my boys to come home.

We were supported by the whole town, and many meals and gift cards showed up at our home. At one point, I asked my mom to tell the church ladies to stop sending food—we couldn't consume it as fast as they cooked it.

When I was discharged from the hospital, I decided that we had to change the boys' visits with their dad. We had been meeting at neutral places, out of town, but I was exhausted and overwhelmed in addition to feeling just plain lousy. I told Jed that he would have to visit the boys in our home, as I was too tired to cart them around.

I went to several neighbors as a courtesy, since I figured they might flip out if they saw Jed's car on our street without an explanation. I told them what time Jed would be visiting our home the next day, and I showed them the IV line sticking out of my arm and wrapped in adhesive. Everyone was wonderful and understanding except Tom and Mary, our neighbors across the street.

Tom began to yell at me, "We don't want him around here. He's a danger to my children."

"He won't be anywhere near your house, Tom. I'm sick, and he will only be in my house."

I waved my arm, with its IV port sticking out, in front of his face. It was hard to miss.

"My boys want to see their dad, and I will be supervising the visit. I just need to be at home," I begged as I started to cry.

He stormed off into his house. Another neighbor came over later to tell me that he had seen Tom yelling at me and had told Tom to leave me alone and mind his own business. This kind neighbor was apologetic because he'd been unsuccessful in calming Tom down.

The next day at the agreed-upon time, Jed pulled up in his car. I looked out and saw Tom standing in his driveway, arms crossed, like a sentry on duty. He stood there looking menacing for the entire ninety minutes or so that Jed was visiting our sons. He looked ridiculous standing guard, as if he thought Jed was going to break into his house in broad daylight and molest his kids. That seemed quite unlikely to me. On the other hand, I understood that he was pissed off. The whole experience changed my relationship with him and his wife. We had always been cordial on the sidewalk. We weren't close, but we used to be neighborly.

We never spoke after that altercation in his driveway. They shot me and my kids dirty looks every time they saw us getting in or out of our car. I found myself looking out the window and timing our trips so I could avoid being outside when Tom and Mary were there. A few months later, they put their house up for sale and moved to another part of town—letting everyone who would listen know that they were moving because of us. The town grapevine buzzed. It seemed that they took every opportunity to gripe about how we had ruined their neighborhood. We were fortunate to have so much support from people, and only one couple was against us.

Interestingly, they moved out of their new neighborhood after only a few years. Word on the street was that they didn't get along with those neighbors either. I felt vindicated when I heard they had moved. I found it interesting that they didn't get along with any of their neighbors, no matter where they lived.

Shortly after receiving the multiple sclerosis diagnosis, I was prescribed a medication that I was going to have to inject daily. The neurologist told me that the initial hurdle would be huge, but that I would soon get used to injecting myself.

My two nurse friends, Patty and Karen, both kindly offered to come to my house and do the injection for me. I liked that idea at first, but then I dismissed it. After all, what would I do if they weren't available? I realized that there would come a day when neither one was able to come over. If it was a daily shot, I was going to have to figure it out and do it myself. It was just another challenge to overcome in my new role as single mom with full custody.

I couldn't catch a break, it seemed, yet I really wanted to take care of my boys. I wanted them to have everything they were supposed to have, even though their dad was gone and their mom had MS. The boys asked if they had to have shots too. They looked very worried as they asked, and were thrilled to hear it was only me.

"Mom, are we going to catch MS or whatever it's called?" Michael asked.

"No sweetie, it's not like a cold. You guys can't catch it."

How can I reassure them? Why do these poor kids have to deal with so much crap?

They soaked in the information I gave them about the illness, and as time went on, the box of my shots that I had to store in the fridge quickly became a fixture. The worst side effect was "injection site reactions"—I would often have a red welt, similar to a bug bite. Sometimes they itched like crazy, but overall the side effects were slight, and I felt fortunate that I could manage them easily.

Luckily, I had been diagnosed with relapsing remitting MS, the milder form of the illness. MS affects the central nervous system, and my neurologist told me that fatigue and stress should be avoided in order to keep the MS under control. That sounded impossible. Fatigue and stress were my constant companions three months after the arrest. Let's face it, at any given moment, either I or one of the boys was near tears and a meltdown, or in the middle of one.

A terrible pattern developed toward the end of the summer. Jed had come to the house to visit the kids. He said goodbye to the boys and got ready to leave, and I dissolved into a puddle of tears. I sat on the steps in the hall and sobbed, and as he approached the front door, I cried even harder. The door meant he was going to leave—and I didn't want a divorced family! I wiped my nose on the sleeve of my T-shirt as he handed me tissues.

"I'm sorry, Di, I don't know what else to say. I am going to leave now. Go in and hang out with the boys." This same routine repeated itself whenever he visited. It was as if a switch got flipped as he walked toward the front door. I would sit on the steps in the living room and begin to cry. I felt weakened by the MS. I was also still very angry with him and exhausted from worry and upset. How was I going to be able to take care of my boys? He was living with his mother, and at times I still hoped that somehow we could put the marriage back together. Most of the time, though, I was furious with him, and I knew our family had been fractured.

When he visited, there was usually no serious conversation about what was going on. Instead he would talk to the boys about what they had done that day at camp. Another frequent topic was how the Red Sox were doing or what movies we had watched. Whenever Jed was there, joining us for a quick meal or chatting while he folded a load of laundry or emptied the dishwasher, we all pretended as if everything were "normal." He never begged me to let him move back in with us, and we never talked about whether we would stay married during these visits with the kids.

The counselor I was seeing told me I had to "break the cycle," so the first night after she and I made the plan, I locked myself in the bathroom when he started to leave. The next time he came over and the visit was ending, I went to my bedroom and called Luisa. I told her what was happening, and she stayed on the phone with me so I wouldn't see him leaving.

After doing this for a few weeks, I broke the pattern of crying when he left. Small successes were huge for me. I noticed I wasn't crying as often. Some nights, I tossed and turned, but at least a few nights a week, I seemed to be able to sleep well for a few hours. I began to feel a little stronger and a bit less overwhelmed.

*To everything there is a season, and a time to
every purpose under heaven.*

—Ecclesiastes 3:1

My mom's first cousin Jim is younger than she is and a decade older than me. I met him for the first time when I was twenty-three, and he moved to New Hampshire after living on the West Coast for many years. He and his wife and children often visited us on holidays while I was in law school and afterward. We chatted frequently in between visits, and my mom and I became very fond of his two little boys.

After I was discharged from the hospital with the MS diagnosis, I kept wondering why I hadn't heard from Jim. It was strange that he hadn't called because we were close by then, and I knew he was worried about me and my boys. The story of Jed's arrest was on the news in New Hampshire as well.

After about a week, I heard from him.

"Hi, Diane, I'm sorry I didn't visit you in the hospital, but the shit hit the fan up here too. Deb left."

"Wait, what happened? What do you mean, she left?" I felt awful for him, as he is one of the kindest and most thoughtful people in my life.

His wife had walked out, leaving him, their thirteen- and sixteen-year-old boys, and her parents who lived in an in-law apartment in his house. Jim was dealing with his own mess and had been waiting, not wanting to call and upset me. *No wonder he didn't want to call me.* Neither of us could believe that we were living this parallel experience simultaneously, both of us dealing with a form of abandonment by our spouses.

In the years after that summer, we have comforted each other many times when one of us is frustrated by the antics of our former spouse and the resulting upset for the kids. We have called each other many times and have taken turns starting the conversation with, "Can I just vent? You won't believe what just happened!"

Whenever Jim and his family would visit, our four boys always enjoyed Wiffle ball, if it was Easter, or a touch football game in the yard at Thanksgiving or Christmas. The cousins would race through dinner and then shed their "fancy" holiday clothes so they could leave the adults at the table and head outside for a down and dirty game.

Michael and Bobby both loved playing football with their cousins and with their buds in our backyard, and they also loved watching football with us on TV. Michael was eager to play Pop Warner football, but we were worried about him getting hurt, so our "family rule" was that you could start tackle football in fourth grade.

That fall after the arrest, when he was going into third grade, Bobby begged me to let him play football, and much to his brother's annoyance, I relented. I thought that football might be a good outlet for his energy. Of course, the "official" sign-up process had ended months before football was to start in late August. Patty's husband assured me that he would find out how to register Bobby, and he did just that.

Bobby was thrilled to get his uniform and helmet as the practices started. The parents usually stayed on the field during practice, another reason why it made sense to let Bobby play instead of making him stand on the sidelines while I watched his brother day after day.

After the first week of practice, the man who served as the volunteer coordinator of the entire Pop Warner program called and asked me to meet him while the kids practiced the following afternoon. I was a wreck. I had no idea what he wanted, but I was sure it had something to do with Jed, and all kinds of things went through my mind while I sweated the meeting. *Was he going to tell me my boys couldn't play because of the media coverage on Jed? Maybe the program didn't want to be part of our crap.* I didn't know what to think.

I was nervous while I waited by the parking lot at the edge of the practice field where we had agreed to meet. He started off by telling me that he and everyone involved in the football program cared about me and my boys. I immediately felt calmer and my breathing steadied; nothing awful was going to happen here.

"The whole staff of volunteer coaches and I will do whatever it takes—we want to give your boys a fun football experience." I began to cry, which seemed to be all I did those days.

"All these guys read the paper, and we all know what's going on. The main reason I wanted to meet with you is to find out if you have a restraining order in place."

"No, no restraining order. He sees the boys, and I'm there to supervise all the visits."

"Okay, well if you did, I'd notify the coaches working with your kids. They would have taken care of everything." I was blown away by this gruff football coach and his willingness to take on our difficult situation. I didn't have a restraining order, but if I did, I know that he would have kept Jed away from us. I came away from the meeting feeling incredibly grateful for his kindness, a football coach angel.

When I was in fourth grade, I received a boxed set of Little House books from my parents for my birthday. I remember thinking that this was the best gift ever. Until that moment, I had never seen a boxed set of books. I looked forward to reading each one in order; having several books meant I knew exactly what I would read next. More importantly, I didn't have to wait to get the next one at the library!

I treasured the set long after the books became dog-eared from multiple readings. I enjoyed moving the box around my room and taking the books in and out of the box nearly as much as reading the stories. Laura Ingalls and her sisters found great joy in choosing a stick of candy at the store when they rode into town with their pa. Their lives were so simple. As an only child, I often had time to myself, and reading was my favorite activity when I was alone. I think getting lost in a story helped me to feel less alone when I couldn't find a kid in the neighborhood to play with.

When my boys were small, they had huge collections of books. They never went to bed without stories and cuddles. When they got to elementary school and brought home the Scholastic book flyers, I encouraged them to order lots and gladly wrote big checks to submit with their order forms. We went through a Cam Jansen series, Biscuit, Captain Underpants, The Boxcar Children, The Hardy Boys, and the much-loved Guinness Book of World Records.

Scholastic always had lots of books about sports and famous athletes. I think we had a copy of everything they put out on those topics for a few years in a row. The books offered were always perfect for their interests at the time, and the prices were reasonable. Santa always brought them lots of books too, because I wanted them to love books as much as I did.

After the arrest, getting the boys to bed was frequently a lengthy process. Often one or both would be upset. There were so many struggles in our lives. Once they were in bed, I felt relieved that they were tucked in and exhausted. Television was not appealing since I had sworn off the news. There was nothing like having your husband featured on the news to make you *not* want to watch it. I began to fall back into reading books.

The stack of fiction piled on my nightstand was a comfort. I knew that after the boys were asleep and I was alone, I would have company in the latest book. I started keeping a list of what I wanted to read next when I heard about a book from a friend or read a review in a magazine. Pretty soon I was reading a book a week, often staying up too late because I was engrossed in the story and didn't want to stop reading. Somehow feeding my passion for a great story began to help me feel like a real person and not just a victim of my husband's crime. The stories helped me escape the trauma that we were living with for just a little while each night. If I had not stayed up late to read fiction during that very difficult time, I probably would have been pacing the house or tossing and turning in bed. Enjoying a complex thriller required me to concentrate and forget about my family's own drama for a while.

My favorite genre was and still is a legal thriller or murder mystery. I love the chase for the bad guy, and I love when the bad guy gets caught. The resolution of the mystery brought comfort, an "all is right with the world" feeling. Sue Grafton, Dennis Lehane, Nelson DeMille, Harlan Coben, and others kept me excellent company.

In addition to reading after I put the boys to bed, I could also read when I went to the hair salon.

Finding time for me to fit in a haircut—or even worse, a cut and color process—required the same amount of logistics, I believe, as Hannibal employed to get his troops across the Alps. Late at night when the boys were asleep, I could pay bills, fold laundry, or talk to a friend on the phone. But hair appointments had to be made in "prime time," between four and seven when the boys had no activities scheduled and I was out of work. On a sunny October day about six months after the arrest, I happily collapsed into the salon chair so my hairdresser could spruce me up a bit. My mom was watching the boys, and I had planned to go to the grocery store after the salon. I latched onto the pile of fluffy magazines in the rack, hoping to enjoy some Hollywood news to distract me from my own woes. I saw an article about a soon-to-be-published book which stopped me in my tracks. Dr. Beth Miller was quoted discussing her book, *The Woman's Book of Resilience: 12 Qualities to Cultivate*.

"Rather than overlooking the pain and difficulty, resilience is actually believing in our ability to bounce back," the article said. I was blown away by the short piece and wanted more. The salon owner let me take the magazine home.

The article stated that Dr. Miller was on staff at UCSF, and as soon as I got home that night, I looked her up. I thought if I could speak to her on the phone, maybe she could teach me how to be resilient so I could get my kids and me through this trying time. I called her and left a message asking if I could make an appointment to speak with her on the phone.

Dr. Miller was kind enough to call me back the next day, and we scheduled a time to talk for an hour later in the week. I was eager to speak with her and practically jumped on the phone when she called. She was kind and warm and asked me to tell her what I was struggling with. When I'd finished relating our saga, she said, "I'm sorry you and your boys are going through this, Diane, but I know you will get through it."

She told me we are all born with resilience, though it can be crushed out of us. But we also can redevelop our resilience when we need to. Dr. Miller encouraged me when she said that just by reaching out for help I was taking a huge step "in the right direction." I had been clutching the phone tightly, but after just a few minutes of conversation, I began to relax. I was comforted to hear that I could actually "grow" resilience in me and my boys. Dr. Miller also said, "People who are willing to ask for help have fewer heart attacks." She encouraged me to take care of myself, because in doing so I would be building resilience.

She said studies have shown that those who survived concentration camps and other atrocities had a reason—such as their faith or their family—that they clung to in order to pull themselves through. Miller explained that I needed to let myself be vulnerable; I had to let the storm go and have its way through me so I could survive. Fighting it would make me brittle. She told me how important it was to let the boys know that we were all okay, even though we were still very upset at times. She said my boys probably worried that they were to blame or that our world was falling apart. She told me to reassure them and to say, "Even though it's taking a long time, we are going to get through this."

Finally, Dr. Miller told me to find small things I could conquer and control right away. Any small, completed task would give me a sense of control and accomplishment. This was the beginning of the process of "growing" resilience. I loved the concept, and Dr. Miller gave me hope, a California doctor angel.

That fall, some of the moms in the neighborhood had signed up for a one-night earring-making class at a local craft store, and they asked me to go. I was so excited when I pictured myself becoming a world-famous jewelry maker in my spare time. I could work from home making fabulous earrings while my boys were at school, and I would make a mint for us. I could become an artist, a designer. Maybe I would reinvent myself and color my hair pink or blue. I thought I would make a great income for my family selling the earrings I learned to make in this low-budget two-hour class. Mostly, though, I was just excited to go out with other moms for a few hours.

When it was time to go, both of my boys got upset and whined, "Why do you have to go out, Mom? Why can't you put us to bed? We don't want Grammy to put us to bed." I felt guilty leaving them. I had not gone out a lot at this point, as all my friends came to the house to see us. It seemed mean to leave the boys upset, but I needed to go out. I wanted to go out.

Nothing is going to be like it was before the arrest.

At the class, I found out that my jewelry-making efforts were not going to earn me a ton of money. Turns out, I was a complete novice, and my earrings looked as if a child had made them.

What I did learn was that going out on a weeknight wasn't smart. I was so tired when I got home that the rest of the morning wake-ups that week were a huge struggle for me. I had only been diagnosed a couple of months before, and I was still learning that I couldn't take care of the boys, the house, and work if I was exhausted.

MS fatigue was very hard to describe to people who didn't have it. It was all-encompassing. I felt it everywhere—even my bones were tired. I often went to bed early and slept until six thirty, and when the alarm went off, I wondered how I could feel exhausted first thing in the morning after a good night's sleep.

One day, some of my coworkers were buying tickets for a week-night concert in Boston. One of the teachers, the "mom" of our school wing, worked hard to convince me to go. "You need to get out of the house," she said. "You need time away from your kids, and you should do something nice for yourself."

"Listen," I said, "I'd love to go with you, but if I go out to a concert on Wednesday night and come home late, the rest of the week will be a disaster at my house."

She kept pushing. "Come on, we all want you to come. You won't have to drive. We'll drive you."

I appreciated her invitation, but I resented her telling me what I needed to do for myself—she had no idea what I felt like day to day with the MS. I stood firm and said I was not going to the concert. Sure, I was disappointed, but I was confident I was making the right choice. Life really was different with MS, and although it sucked in some ways, it felt good to take control. I knew I needed to choose my outside activities carefully to give myself the best outcome.

After the show, everyone said they had missed me, which was sweet. I was happy at home that night.

I had learned by then that if I got to bed early and read for a while, I could function at work. If I stayed out late, the MS fatigue would kick my butt and make it a struggle for me to do what I needed to do. It wasn't easy to get the boys and me ready and show up at work ready to teach at 7:25 every morning. I was frustrated when people said, "But you look fine." Since I didn't look sick, it was hard for people to understand my condition, but my fatigue was ever present.

One sunny fall day, I took the boys to the Topsfield Fair when we were off from school. We munched on junk food and roamed around the fairgrounds. We spent the most time in the baby animal exhibits. Something about the little fuzzy bunnies cuddling touched our hearts. The boys begged for a pet, and I agreed that we could get two bunnies in the spring.

I kept us busy. We were always heading out somewhere on an adventure, because if we were home, the boys tended to squabble. Getting out, running around, and doing "stuff" seemed to make us all happier and calmer. We went to local museums, Quincy Market, and the aquarium with free passes from the library. I also kept us busy with family playdates—visiting Luisa and her kids, Trish and hers, or our friends in town. What worked best was if we got out of the house early in the day when I had energy; even if I was tired, I could enjoy the day knowing we'd be back at home cuddling and watching a movie by evening.

Free activities helped the budget, but I worried constantly about paying the mortgage. In the winter, the heating oil bill was going to be an added worry. The kids' activities, music lessons, sports fees, cleats, and uniforms were also regular expenses each season. I prided myself on never telling them that they had to skip a sport because we didn't have the money.

The school system paid my salary on Fridays. Usually on the prior Monday, I had the bills written out ready to send, even though the money wasn't going to be deposited until Thursday night. It seemed like there were often just a few dollars in the checking account because as soon as the salary went in, it went right out for bills and expenses.

After hauling produce with Gerry for a few months, Jed wanted a more secure and better-paying job. His options were very limited, though, due to the pending criminal case. In the fall, Jed convinced his mom to buy him a business so he would have a secure income. She spent several hundred thousand dollars and bought him a small café that served breakfast and lunch and was located in an industrial park. He didn't know anything about running a business, but he shadowed the seller for a few days and learned how much to buy at Costco and how much to spend on soft drinks. To his credit, I guess, he knew he would never teach or coach again, and he wanted a job and an income stream. I'm certain that unless she bought this business, he would not have found a job. Who would hire an alleged sex offender whose arrest was all over the news?

Money was always on my mind, and I had an almost unnatural fear of the car breaking down. It was a twofold issue: I was worried that the boys and I would be stranded somewhere if the car died, but I also worried about how to manage an unexpected, expensive car repair bill. I knew I would have to put the payment on a credit card. As a practical matter, my fears were a bit unfounded. After all, we could have walked to school and work if we needed, or gotten rides with friends if our car was not functioning. I think having a one-car household scared me because it was another reminder that we were alone and without backup. My car was also a terrible reminder of how I had heard about his arrest. I could look at the car and remember all the emotion surrounding the event. Two-parent households could survive with one car if the other was in the shop, but I couldn't go from one to none. The same fear met me when I thought of house repairs. *How would I pay for stuff when it didn't work?* I blamed everything on the arrest, but even if we had still been together, a big repair bill would have been a challenge for us. We hadn't had much disposable income even then.

Jed had some less-than-helpful ideas about money and extra income for us. When he moved to his mom's house, he didn't take any furniture from our house. A few months after the arrest, he suddenly remembered that he had left an old Ping-Pong table in the shed. We had never set it up in all the years we'd been married, so it wasn't in great shape. He called me one day and suggested that the boys could sell it and "make a lot of money."

I was annoyed, but the boys and I trudged out to the shed and moved all the junk that was piled up in front of the Ping-Pong table. At last, buried under lawn furniture, broken shovels, and the lawn mower—there it was, folded in half and partly faded. We pulled that table out and discovered that it would not fold flat, as it had warped from so many years in the damp shed. No big fortune there.

A few weeks later, we went through the same song and dance with an old desk that he had left behind when he went to his mom's.

"Diane, I think you should let the boys sell my old desk so they can make some money. I don't have room for it," he announced on the phone one night.

Not so much. The desk was mammoth and weighed a ton. It had been destined for the junkyard when a school he'd worked at years earlier was renovating. He'd asked if he could have it and was allowed to take it.

I was angry that, instead of working more, he was spending time kidding himself about the value of his old junk. Money was a constant worry, and it seemed that everywhere I looked, I was reminded of how tight the household budget was. After the desk fiasco, I yelled at him on the phone, "Why don't you get another job so you can earn more money to help us instead of itemizing your stuff and foolishly thinking it's worth selling? The desk won't bring in enough to pay a single utility bill. You are such an idiot!"

Then he went from selling to shopping. In November, Jed arrived for a visit with the boys carrying a large, bulky item that looked like a statue. When I opened the door to let him in, I had to sidestep so he could fit by me. When I looked closely, I saw that it was a CD holder in the shape of an Egyptian god, very tacky and strange. *What the hell is that?*

"Look, I got this on sale at T.J. Maxx. It was marked down to seventy-five dollars," he proudly announced. "It will look great in the living room and can store the kids' video games."

Not loving this in my living room.

I didn't want to have a fight about it, especially in front of the kids, but I figured I needed to set him straight, or he might keep buying things I didn't want. I had to say no right away.

"Thanks, I know you think that this is helpful, but I'm not crazy about it. I'm sure you like it because it looks historical, but I don't think it matches the rest of the house. Would you please return it?"

Freaking strange.

"And please don't buy anything for me or the boys for *our* house unless you ask me first." He hung his head like a small kid who had been reprimanded. *He just doesn't get it,* I thought for the thousandth time. *I can barely stay afloat over here working and struggling to get the three of us to our appointments and he is wandering the aisles of T.J. Maxx looking for crap on sale to bring us. What the hell?*

My boys touched my heart on the day after Thanksgiving that year. When I woke up, the kids were already downstairs with the newspaper spread out between them on the couch.

"Good morning, sweeties," I said as I hugged them.

Michael grabbed the paper that they had been reading and threw a pillow over it. I chuckled because they were both working hard to make sure that I didn't see what they were reading. About an hour later I heard them upstairs talking, and I heard coins rattling. Suddenly they were racing back downstairs and heading outside.

"Mom, we are going to ride our bikes," said Bobby. "Don't worry, we're fine."

I was pretty sure that my kids were on their way to buy me something for Christmas. I knew that they had been reading holiday ads in the newspaper, and I also knew that the noise I'd heard was the sound of them emptying their piggy banks. I was blinking back the tears as I looked out the window and watched them bike up the street. *What thoughtful kids I have.* They were gone a short time, and I was folding laundry when Maria called me. "I have your boys," she said.

"What? They're biking to the store."

"They called me because they had a big box, and they couldn't ride their bikes because the box kept hitting the wheels, no matter who tried to carry it. I picked them up, and their bikes are in my van. Act surprised on Christmas."

The kids had ridden to the electronics store in our neighborhood and pooled their money to buy a DVD player so I could watch movies in my bedroom. I wish I'd been able to witness the transaction as it happened, my two boys counting up a pile of change and dollar bills to pay the bill.

Life is all about how you handle Plan B.

—Anonymous

Eleven months after my dad passed away, we had to face Christmas. Things were still bleak. My dad had loved Christmas and had established many traditions, including buying a huge box of holly each year and making small bunches for me to deliver to all the neighbors. He wrote a personal note on every Christmas card, and then there was Christmas Eve caroling, which he organized in the neighborhood. Our first Christmas without him was going to be terrible; there was no way my mom and I could do all the things he did to make Christmas wonderful. We also missed him, and it didn't feel like there was much reason to celebrate without him. My mom was going to work her hostess job on Christmas. I was angry about that; it seemed like she wanted to pretend it wasn't Christmas since my dad wasn't there. I was still there, but she didn't want to celebrate with me. It's not as if she was going to earn big money that day, but that was her excuse, that we needed the money. I felt like she was bailing out on me.

On Christmas Eve, she didn't get out of bed. I watched movies. My friends were amazing and hosted me on Christmas day while my mom worked. Luisa and Tricia each invited me to be with their families. In the morning, I put on a dressy holiday outfit and drove to Luisa's house. I spent half the day there and then drove to Tricia's grandmother's house for the rest of the day. I remember fighting back tears at times, but I did feel welcome and was warmly greeted by both families. Tricia's young cousin Ro, a teenager at the time, had a gift for me. I remember thinking, *Wow, everyone in her family knew I was coming and that I was coming alone.* I knew they felt sorry for me. My mom worked all day. How strange not to be with my own family on Christmas, and thank God for my dear friends.

When my dad passed, I was amazed at both the kindness of many people, and the ineptitude of a few at expressing their condolences. One acquaintance said, "I didn't want to bring up your dad and remind you and make you sad." *How dumb! Do you think I am thinking of anything else right now?* I think they were afraid to bring it up—maybe they worried that I would get upset, and they didn't want to deal with that.

I would have appreciated them asking me how I was and being direct about it. I was twenty-one when my dad died, and after the funeral I made a commitment to myself. As a way of honoring my dad, whenever I heard about a death, I would step up and ask how I could help. I would be bold about looking the survivor in the eye and asking in a meaningful way, "What can I do and what do you need?" I would be sure to send a card, make a donation, and go to the wake or the service because it really did matter when people showed up to celebrate a life.

In the future, I'd be the person who asked somebody, "How are you?" and would not shy away from the topic of the loss of their loved one. My mom often said that two or three weeks seemed to be the cutoff. A couple of weeks after the funeral, people stop sending you casseroles, the phone stops ringing, and people resume their ordinary routines. They expect you to be "over" the death, and routines go back to normal except for the immediate family of the loved one. Their adjustment to the loss is just beginning.

For a while right after my dad passed away, we were swept up in the business of thank-you notes, neighbors dropping by, and not having to cook anything. Then it all stopped. After our experience, my mom always reached out to people a month and longer after the funeral of their loved one. She remembered that was when people had stopped calling her. She sent cards and made calls long after the service was over, and when she did, people always said, "Thank you, I think everyone else forgot."

The boys and I were so fortunate because the support we received after the arrest went on and on, for months and years, not merely weeks. This is because my friends are extraordinarily caring, thoughtful, and kind people. I am blessed.

Right around Christmas, seven months after the arrest, I became overwhelmed while working at school one day. I don't know what set me off, but I think it was one of the children talking about the upcoming holiday and how excited she was.

"Suzie, what are you hoping to get from Santa?" Annie was whispering to her friend during circle time. *It's everywhere. I can't stop thinking about Christmas even for a second. It's going to be so hard this year.* For the rest of the morning, I had to fight back tears, but I managed to hold it together. I didn't want to cry at work in front of the students. I made it through the end of that class, but as soon as the children were dismissed, I practically raced out of the room and down the hall to the ladies' room. I couldn't hold back the tears any longer. I grabbed the door to open it, slammed it shut, and locked it behind me, and the next thing I knew, I was on the bathroom floor sobbing. I couldn't believe that Christmas was still coming. I had always loved the holiday, but we were barely surviving; how could we possibly celebrate? It just seemed like we would always be sad and always be in crisis. The Christmas carols on the radio were painful to hear.

That first Christmas without Jed at home felt strange; the boys were excited about their gifts, but there was also a lot of sadness. One night while getting ready for bed, I had a spontaneous idea: we would start a new tradition of "early presents." I'd been trying to find a way to cheer the boys up because it seemed like we were just going through the motions of the Christmas season, and most days we were still not happy.

We had just finished planning when to buy our tree. The boys wanted to know how we would put it up, since their dad had always hauled it from the roof of the car into the house. We wondered how we would lug the boxes of ornaments down from the attic ourselves. It seemed that every time we thought about our old traditions, they missed their dad even more.

While the boys were brushing their teeth, I went to my closet, pulled out a couple of their small gifts, and wrapped them quickly in white tissue paper. Christmas was still two weeks away, and I hadn't taken the Christmas paper out of the attic yet.

"Come into my room after you brush your teeth. I have an early present surprise!"

When the water in the boys' bathroom stopped running, I could hear them talking. "What did you say, Mom?" asked Michael with a mouthful of toothpaste.

"Early present surprise!"

I didn't want to send them to bed sad and upset and missing their dad. It seemed silly, but I had the urge to bury them with fun gifts in the hope it would make them happy. I knew that I couldn't afford a lot of early gifts—it wasn't practical or sensible—but one little present early I could do.

The boys climbed on my bed and looked excited as I held my hands behind my back to hide the presents. They tore into the little packages as soon as I handed them out.

"Oh cool! Red Sox pencils," they squealed with delight. I was happy that they were excited about this very small gift that helped us end the day in an upbeat way. Most importantly, though, we had established a new tradition for ourselves. It got to be a joke because we would ask each other nearly every day, "Is it time for an early present?"

About a week later, the three of us got home after a busy afternoon. I opened the fridge to take out the chicken so I could start making a quick stir-fry dinner. This meal was one of our favorites, and I also loved it because it was blissfully easy and quick to prepare. Unfortunately, I had forgotten to take the chicken out of the freezer, so I had nothing ready, and the three of us were starving. *Ugh, fantastic start to the evening.*

While I was trying to figure out what I could make instead, the boys began to poke and annoy each other instead of doing their homework, which I had told them to start.

First I heard, "Quit kicking me."

Then it quickly escalated to, "Mom, tell him to stop." This was followed by many variations on both statements from both kids.

"Can you two cut it out? I told you to do your homework. Give me a break!" After yelling at the kids for the umpteenth time about less arguing and more homework, I finally lost it. I sat on the couch and cried. It was almost Christmas, and I was exhausted. I had to get dinner on the table and do paperwork, and the boys were plucking every last nerve. I was bitchy and cranky.

While I was on the couch with tissues in hand, the boys stopped bickering, whispered to one another, and ran out of the kitchen and up the stairs. I heard a door slamming and some rustling of bags. Two minutes later, my cherubs were patting me on the back and saying, "Don't cry, you need an early present to cheer you up, Mom."

Maria had taken them out shopping for me. She brought them to the nicest gift store in town and went wild buying me gifts. They told me afterward about her kindness; one of them would pick up an item and turn it over to see the price, and she would say, "Don't worry about the price. Your mom will love it. Put it in my basket." They had chosen a paperweight for my desk, a candle, and it seemed like one of every beautiful item in the store. She had paid for everything. As I was drying my tears, I opened a bottle of hand lotion, the best I had ever received.

Early presents went a long way toward cheering us up. We ordered a pizza to be delivered, the boys stopped fighting and did their homework, and I paid the bills. We were learning how to cope with our upset and still move forward. There were still many more hurdles ahead, including the uncertainty of the outcome of Jed's pending criminal case.

One of the many things that my mother-in-law shelled out money to her son for was the cost of his legal defense. Part of the defense attorney's recommendation was expert testimony from a mental health professional.

Dr. C had been retained by the defense, and Jed met with her several times so she could analyze him and testify on his behalf in court. She had treated many other alleged sex offenders charged with crimes. The hope was that she would meet with Jed, examine him, and her findings would be helpful to his court case.

In January, I was given the opportunity to meet with her and read her findings. I believe Jed hoped my meeting with her would answer all my questions, so he wouldn't have to explain things to me himself. Much easier to let her be the messenger. I think he also felt he would earn some brownie points for letting me speak with her.

Dr. C's office was near Tricia's house, a good hour from where we lived. I took a personal day from school, told the boys I had a doctor's appointment, and told Bobby that he would not see me in school. I dropped the boys off and fought the traffic to get to Trish's house, and together we drove to Dr. C's office.

The doctor greeted us and brought us into an empty office. She gave me her reports to read and said she would come back later and answer my questions.

I took notes, of course, about what I read and about her answers to my many questions.

At this point in time, I was pretty sure that our marriage was over, but I still held out hope for some sort of miracle. I didn't want to tell my sons that their parents were getting divorced.

According to the report, there were a few issues that she had noted about his personality, but the most important piece of information was her statement that he was "coming to terms with accepting his homosexuality." *Wait, what—he's gay?* I went out to the receptionist and told her I was ready to talk to the doctor.

She came back in with a kind expression on her face, pulled up a chair, and sat next to me instead of sitting at her desk across from me. As I looked at her, I could feel myself starting to cry. Her office was chilly and I was shivering. It was yet another moment—there had been so many since May—when I wondered, *What happened to my life and why do I have to be here, doing this right now?* She answered many of my questions with statements like, "You deserve better. You should have a happy relationship." In other words, I should give up this marriage because it would never work—she said his head might be in it, but in her opinion, he really wasn't capable. I found it hard to concentrate and kept staring at the pattern in the carpet.

I felt like she was Jed's messenger; he didn't want to tell me himself that our marriage was over. By allowing me to meet with her, he knew that she would break the news to me. Once I realized it, I thought it was cowardly of him.

The crux of the meeting was when I asked Dr. C if she thought Jed was dealing appropriately with reality; I felt that he had not owned up to walking out on us. He had told me on several occasions that he wasn't going to New Hampshire to have sex with the minor. He was just trying to "help" him and talk to him. *Come on, really?* The email content printed in the newspapers was very explicit. He needed to own this. She told me that the drive to New Hampshire was escapism for him. She had concluded and would testify that he was not a pedophile.

I leaned on Trish as we walked out of the office, and I said, "A hired gun will say anything."

That night on the phone, I was yelling at Jed. "We were married, then you went after a kid, now you're gay? What's it going to be next week?" I screamed at him. I believed that a healthy gay man would not desire a fourteen-year-old. In fact, a gay friend of mine said, "We don't want him on our team. That isn't who we are." The gay label seemed like a cover story to me for his deeper demons, and I didn't buy it.

After that, Patty wisely told me not to let him come to the house anymore. "He can't have the privilege of hanging out at your house and 'helping' by doing laundry," she said. From then on, he picked up our kids in the driveway and took them out to eat or to a park to play catch.

Once I had met with Dr. C, I felt confident that I had to move forward with the divorce. There was no way to repair our shattered marriage. The first step was letting the boys know. I told Jed what time to show up, and the four of us had a very awkward "meeting" at the kitchen table.

"I have something to tell you," I began. "It's very sad, and it's hard for me to say it, but we are going to get divorced. Dad has decided that he does not want to be part of this family. He wants to live a different kind of life." The boys were blinking back tears, and I was crying. Jed kept looking at the floor; he didn't have much to say. Neither of us said anything about him being gay.

When he left, I followed him to the sidewalk. I could feel myself sweating, my heart was pounding, and I was so angry I felt I was going to explode, Incredible Hulk-style. As the anger grew, it was scary. He was digging through his pocket looking for his car keys. I heard my neighbor's garage door opening, and farther down the street, a dog barked. I knew people might hear me but I didn't care. I screamed, "How can you be so selfish?" He said nothing, just stared at me.

"Stop thinking with your dick and act like a real father. How dare you leave us?" I yelled.

He began to walk away from me toward the driver's side door of his car. *Oh no*, I thought, *you can't walk away*. He needed to stand there and take it until I was done yelling at him. He was leaving to go play on one of the many recreational sport teams he had joined. I was facing an evening of homework, laundry, house cleaning, and doubtless some tears. He had left his family and now had a new lifestyle full of gay sport teams and bars and who-knows-what-else. I was left behind in the trenches to raise our children by myself. Every meal they needed, every activity they were involved in, every single thing was all me. I needed him to stay and listen while I vented. The problem was that he apparently felt differently. Without saying anything, he opened his car door, got in, shut the door, and started the engine. He was going to leave. My last thread of propriety dissolved and my screaming got much louder. I was incensed that he was going to drive away when I wasn't done yelling at him.

I wanted to make sure that he couldn't leave, so I began to pound the windshield with my fist. I believed I could—and I most certainly wanted to—break his windshield. I kept pounding the glass, as he sat in the driver's seat silently looking at me. My hand hurt; in fact it hurt a lot as I continued pummeling. I was getting more upset because even though I was giving it everything I had, of course, I couldn't break the glass, not even a hairline crack.

I'm sure the neighbors saw me; we were out there for a while. I never gave it a thought. I was so caught up in my task that my mom startled me when she appeared on the sidewalk.

She quietly spoke to me, suggesting that I stop yelling and banging. "Think of the boys. You don't want them to see you carrying on like this," she said. My mom had her hand on my arm, gently at first, but then she started to pull me into a hug so I had to back away from the car. I wanted to keep banging; I was nowhere near done unleashing my anger on this man who had destroyed our family. I was just beginning to cover all the awful things I wanted to say to him. It felt great to scream at him.

"You are so fucking selfish! How can you walk out on our sons? I don't want to be a single mother so you can lead a gay lifestyle."

Again, my mom tried to persuade me to go inside. When I looked at my husband through the windshield, he looked back at me with pity. I was devastated. I didn't want his pity; somehow it would have been easier if he'd been mad at me. My angry performance had accomplished nothing. I don't know what I was thinking—I must have known I couldn't break the windshield—but at that moment, I was consumed with rage and intent on breaking something.

But in the end, the car was undamaged, he drove away, we were getting divorced, and I was officially a single mom. The next morning, a huge bruise on my hand was the souvenir of my fury on the sidewalk.

*Never let the fear of striking out keep you
from playing the game.*

—Babe Ruth

In 1975 the Red Sox went to the playoffs. Venues are required to hire and pay for a police presence at an event, and these jobs provide overtime for police officers because they work them in addition to their regularly assigned shifts. That summer, my dad did a lot of detail work at Fenway. Whenever he had an afternoon game, I would alert my buddies in the neighborhood, and we would pile into our family station wagon and ride into Fenway with my dad. It was very exciting because we had to be there early so my dad could work. We loved being in the park early to watch batting practice. In those days, it was just a few dollars for a bleacher ticket, and there were always plenty available, even on game day. One of my fondest memories of Fenway Park is the last day of that regular season in 1975 as our Sox finished first in the American League East. When the crowds began to climb over the railings onto the field in celebration, one of the kids in the neighborhood began to start his climb. His brother grabbed his shirt and said, "Stop! Do you want Mr. Stelfox to be mad at you?" The kid who was thinking about jumping onto the field stopped and turned around to look at us; we pointed to my dad who was in uniform, looking stern. He was facing the seats, and he was grabbing spectators as they ran by him so they couldn't run onto the field. No way were any of us going to try to run out onto the field! The kid looked chagrined and came down off the railing.

We left the park and waited for my dad at the car, talking over one another as we reviewed the entire game. Our Sox were headed to the postseason, and we were elated! I was so proud of my dad being on the field that day, keeping order at Fenway and keeping everyone safe. I was relieved that none of the neighborhood kids got into trouble!

Eleven months after the arrest, the boys and I vacationed with Patty and her family. Patty had researched and found out that the Red Sox were playing in Toronto, and she had built a trip around the games. We happily joined in. The trip made me think of my dad and all our games at Fenway. Patty's three boys and my two were good friends, and the kids were excited to be going on a trip with their buddies. Her husband—what a saint he was!—drove the giant van we rented. The five boys decided before we had even left Massachusetts that they wanted to be on the local television station's broadcast, which often featured Sox fans attending away games. Michael called NESN from the back seat of the van while the other boys leaned in for support. He told them that we were big Sox fans, traveling to Canada for the game. He left the section number of our seats on the voicemail message, and the three adults figured that would be the end of it. The children were ecstatic when the NESN reporter showed up during the pregame batting practice to interview them.

"Hi, guys, where are you traveling from?" the young reporter asked.

"Boston!" they all shouted.

"Who's Michael? We got a phone message."

Michael jumped out of his seat and eagerly responded to the questions about our hometown and the length of our stay in Canada.

The boys were all decked out in Red Sox gear, and Patty had brought body paint. Each kid had one letter of "GO SOX" painted on his belly. They were psyched!

The interview was fun, but the glory came when we got home and everyone we knew told the boys that they had watched the game and seen their interview. The boys were local celebrities, and this gave them big bragging rights in school!

Someone in Patty's family had taped the interview, and we laughed many times when we heard the comments from the guys in the booth who were calling the play-by-play, right after the segment with our boys.

"What a trip, driving five kids from Boston. I'm glad I wasn't in that car."

"Yup, me too. Those parents are crazy."

What a memorable vacation, even though it took me months to pay off the credit card.

One of the biggest homework meltdowns we ever had was over a worksheet Bobby had to do one night. He had a math teacher he didn't like and he was struggling to grasp the material. He couldn't figure out the assignment and neither could I. Michael wasn't home to help, and before long both Bobby and I were both in tears. I told him I would write the teacher a note explaining that we had tried and just couldn't get it done, and he melted down. "She is so mean, Mom,"

he said. "She will be mad if you write a note." *Well, isn't this dandy,* I thought. *My kid's upset, I'm upset, and I can't help him figure out a dumb math sheet. If we weren't in such a mess, I wouldn't have this problem.* Some days I blamed everything on Jed's crime, but later I learned that many families had struggled with that math teacher and her homework assignments.

During times like these, when I was there to help my sons with their homework, I wondered how I would ever leave my special ed job and return to work as an attorney. We were busy with social worker appointments, plus the orthodontist, religious education, sports, and homework after school. I actually enjoyed driving the boys around each day. Once my school day ended, I had a five- or six-hour shift of chauffeuring my kids around, then we had dinner and did homework. How could I get them everywhere they needed to be if I got home at six every night? And let's face it, with some law jobs, six o'clock was probably entirely too optimistic.

Stu, the principal of the school where I worked, pulled me into his office about a year after the arrest. He suggested, out of the blue, that I get my teacher certification. He said I could teach, earn more than I was getting as an aide, and have the same vacation schedule as the boys. I was very flattered but initially very quick to tell him that I thought his idea was crazy.

I said to him, "More school? Do you have any idea how much schooling I already have?" (It was four years of college plus three of law school.) "I couldn't possibly start another round of higher education." How did he think I would find the time to go to school, and how would I pay for it? It seemed to be a crazy idea, but I was pleased that he'd suggested it. His school was amazing, and I thought his staff was terrific.

His voice kept ringing in my ears, thankfully. I was getting really fed up with the terrible salary I was receiving as an aide and feeling stronger emotionally. I thought I should explore the steps and find out what I would need to do in order to get the teacher certification, if only to be respectful of my principal who had been so kind to encourage me. I thought I would look into it, and then I could at least report back to him. I was just going on a fact-finding mission, as I didn't really think I would end up teaching.

I asked the assistant superintendent for a meeting. She oversaw special education in our town and kindly agreed to meet with me. I was admiring the beautiful plaques and wall hangings with inspiring quotes in her office when she came in and introduced herself. *This woman is glamorous*, I thought, feeling frumpy in my out-of-date suit that was left over from my lawyering days. She was tall and wore a gorgeous black dress, a long strand of pearls, and lots of perfectly applied makeup. She had to be in her sixties based on her diplomas but looked twenty years younger. I was intimidated, but she graciously greeted me.

After a quick handshake, I jumped right in. "If I wanted to teach special education, what would I need to do? I love being an assistant, but I'm not earning enough money."

Before she could answer, her secretary came in with coffee for us.

"You would need to get your master's degree and also take the state teacher qualifying tests. But tell me, why do you want to stop practicing law? Tell me what kind of law you practiced."

We spent most of our meeting with her asking me about my law career, and she was very kind and supportive. She told me that she wished she had a law degree, and I think she thought I was nutty to give it up but was too polite to say so.

Ironically, the middle school principal, who was Michael's principal at the time, saw me in the waiting area as I was leaving and asked what I was doing there.

She kindly said, "I would hire you right now if I could."

In May, I took and passed the two state teacher tests; it was a long, grueling day, but I took both in the same sitting. Later, I found out that nobody takes both in the same day, but I needed to get them done. I was fairly sure that I wouldn't pass, but I had to try since Stu's voice was always in my head: "You should get certified." When I passed both, I began to think his plan might actually work.

The university was only ten minutes from our house, and their education programs were fantastic. That summer, while the boys were at day camp for eight weeks—thanks to my mom who paid that huge bill—I took the first four classes for the master's degree in education. I enjoyed the intellectual stimulation and the camaraderie of my classmates. After working as a special ed assistant for two years, I had learned a lot on the job, but the master's level classes taught me much more. Initially I worried that I was too old to start a new program and was delighted to meet students of all ages, many older than I was!

My parents valued education, and from the time I was a little girl, I knew they expected me to go to college and also that they would do whatever it took financially to get me there. My father attended college and earned a bachelor's degree as an adult when he was a Boston police officer, thanks to a program offered by the Justice Department in the seventies that allowed police officers to earn a college degree.

My dad worked full time and attended college full time. He loved going to school and felt it was a privilege. My mom had earned an associate's degree when she was in her twenties, and as an adult she too returned to school. She attended college at night and earned a bachelor's degree just before I completed mine. The importance my parents placed on education, along with their work ethic, was drilled into my head from a young age.

When I was a sophomore in college, the dorms were packed tight, and my room had been carved out of an old student lounge to accommodate the crowds. My room and the one next door lacked the built-in shelves and closet that the other rooms had, and a flimsy wall separated the two rooms. Our rooms were also significantly smaller than the rest of the rooms in the dorm. There was something wrong with the outside wall too, and a gap at the top where the wall met the ceiling was big enough that we could see daylight streaming through. We could also feel the breeze when we put our hand there. When my parents saw the room, my dad immediately took measurements so he could make shelves for my roommate and me. He delivered them a week later.

When my parents overheard some of the other parents complaining about the size of the room and the crack in the wall and the lack of shelves, they pulled me aside and shared their very different thoughts. We stood out in the quad so we could talk privately. Since they went to college at night as adults, they were thrilled that I could be a full-time student living in a dorm.

"Listen, bunny, your room is just fine. We worked hard so you could be enrolled as a student and live on campus. Learn as much as you can and concentrate on your schoolwork. Your mother and I didn't have the chance to go to college full time, and we are happy that you have the chance," my dad said. It was clear that nobody from our family was going to contact the administration to complain about the room. I was there to study and to learn.

While I was working on my master's, I first heard the phrase "lifelong learner." It clicked in my head, because certainly my parents had instilled it in me, even though I hadn't had a name for it.

As I was finishing up my first four classes, I got a call in August from the town hall. They had an opening in seventh grade, Michael's grade, for a special education teacher. They were adding a new position, and the assistant superintendent said, "I'm going to be your fairy god-mother today. I have a job for you."

"But I just started the master's program. I'm not ready," I said.

"You passed the teacher tests, you're a lawyer, and you have been an assistant for two years. We will need you to finish the degree, but you'll be fine." My next thought was, *Poor Michael. He is going to have his mom near him all day.*

What a huge moment, landing a new job and knowing that I could have snow days and the school vacations off. How incredibly kind this school district staff was to give me this opportunity after what my husband did, dragging their school system through the mud of the media with his arrest. I was terrified at the thought of starting this new job, yet it felt wonderful to know that I would be working close to home, in Michael's school, which was the school Bobby would be in the following year. How strange that I was now on the teaching staff of the district that Jed had just left.

Once again, my army of friends stepped up. Marylee said I could drop Bobby in the morning at her house since my day would start earlier than his. She would bring him to the elementary school with her son when it was time to go. Linda said she would pick up Bobby in the afternoon when she got her daughter, and I could collect him at her house when I was done for the day. Free child care twice a day. My friends were so kind.

Michael and I could commute together, or he could take the bus. As a seventh grader, he did not need as much childcare as his fourth-grade brother. Both boys seemed excited that I was going to be a teacher.

"Good job, Mom," Bobby said. We were sitting at the kitchen table and I was telling them what I knew so far. "What classes will you have? Can I see your classroom?"

"I'll have orientation first, and then a few days of meetings before you start school. Maybe you guys can help me set up the room."

"Oh cool, can we go in early to see everything before school starts?" Michael asked.

They were proud of me, I think. Neither of them ever complained that I was in their middle school with them, all day every day.

In September, right after I started teaching special education, the kids and I went to Florida for four days. A bunch of families in our town had planned the trip to Orlando to coincide with the Jewish holidays when we would all be off from school. I wanted desperately to join them but wasn't sure how to swing it financially. In the end, I sold my wedding and engagement rings to pay for the trip.

I stood at the jewelry counter at the store, hoping to get lots of money for my rings while also feeling sad about selling them. It wasn't a pawn shop, but it felt like one because it was in a rough neighborhood, and the store was dark and small. You definitely wouldn't go here to buy a decent piece of jewelry. The owner wasn't very friendly when I walked in, and I reminded myself that I had to negotiate and not take his first offer. I thought that letting go of the rings might help bring "closure," whatever that meant, but it was actually hard to hand them over to the jeweler. It seemed very final. The marriage was over, and I was trying to eke some money out of these same rings that I had treasured and worn every day. Standing at the jewelry counter tapping on the glass case while the owner studied my rings, I felt mercenary and cold—this was a business deal. I needed the money, and I tried not to think about the rings. I had to let them go. What helped was wanting to go on the trip with my kids, and the sale made that possible.

We had a blast in Florida, and taking the trip marked the beginning of a new start for the three of us.

*Some days doing "the best we can" may still fall short of what
we would like to be able to do, but life isn't perfect—
on any front—and doing what we can with what we have
is the most we should expect of ourselves or anyone else.*

—Anonymous

I continued working on my master's degree at night, taking one or
two classes each semester. My mom would feed the boys dinner and
get them to bed on the nights I had school. Class nights made for a
long day, but I actually loved going. All my classmates and my pro-
fessors were teaching children during the day, and I found my school
to be a wonderful support in my role as a new teacher.

At times, juggling the schoolwork that I had to complete for my
master's was tricky due to the hectic schedule the boys and I had. On
one weekend, I was facing a deadline for a project that was due for
an online class. Michael was going to be away for the weekend with
a friend, and I wondered how Bobby and I could enjoy the weekend
since I was going to have to be at the computer in our family room
for hours at a time. I got the brilliant idea to let him pick out a new

Lego—he was really into them then, so we went to Toys R Us, and he spent quite a while choosing which one to buy. It wasn't his birthday, so he was excited to be getting a new toy for no reason. I explained that while he was putting it together, I would be working on the computer for my class.

The weekend flew by, and we spent almost all of it in the family room. On Saturday night as I was making us a quick dinner, I said, "Bud, this is awesome. Mommy is getting so much work done. Thank you for playing quietly."

"I'm having fun, Mom. I never spent a whole entire day doing Legos before. I just take a break when I need a Goldfish snack."

I finished the whole project by Sunday morning, and Bobby was totally wrapped up in his Legos on the floor next to me, assembling pieces and then sections while I typed. We were both pleased with our progress. I was thrilled that he was able to stay busy so I could work, and I was glad that we worked side by side all weekend.

When you are a single parent, you don't have a partner to bounce things off of or to plan with. My mom and my friends were always helpful, but sometimes I needed to find solutions for my kids and me without farming them out to a sitter. You have to be resourceful as a parent, and even more so when you are a single parent. You don't have another built-in person to cover when your workload increases at the office or if you don't feel well. At times, I worried that I wasn't enough, but this weekend of writing the paper with Legos was a milestone for us. Creative planning got the work done. Hopefully I could keep figuring out how to do everything that two parents were supposed to do.

After talking with our pediatrician and not getting any helpful ideas about how to deal with my sons' problems, I'd called John. He was a social worker in town who had seen many kids and families. I knew him slightly because I had contacted him a few months before the arrest. My boys were battling at times at home, so he had seen us for just a couple of visits to try and rein in the negative behavior. But that sibling rivalry and fighting over toys was very minor in comparison to our new issues. Anyway, I called John, and when he called me back, he said he was sorry. He had read the paper and seen the news so he knew all about the reason for my call. I told him that my pediatrician had not been helpful, and I was crying as I asked him to please help us.

"I think we need to see you. Can you please help me take care of my boys?"

I will never forget his kind response: "Diane, I have never dealt with anything like this before. It would be a privilege to help you and the boys. You don't deserve this."

We saw John regularly, maybe hundreds of times in total. Sometimes just me, usually both boys, sometimes alone and sometimes together. After a while, I learned not to tell my boys ahead of time when they had an appointment because inevitably they would whine and complain and say that they didn't want to go see him.

When we had a meeting set with John, I would pick up the boys, and on the back seat I would have a juice box and what the boys called a "treaty" snack, something unhealthy that I would not usually have in the house. Quickly they caught on and when they saw the snack, they knew we were going to see John. It was my way of offering them a small bribe. I knew it was hard to go and talk with John about difficult issues, but I was committed to the process. I felt that having counseling in place was the best way I could ensure that my boys would come out of the mess created by their dad.

There were weeks when we didn't have an appointment with John, but most weeks we did. John was interviewed by the guardian ad litem when Jed was fighting for unsupervised visitation. A few times I had a phone appointment with him when we had a crisis and I couldn't get in to see him. John was there through every aspect of the legal case. When I had a tough issue, I would meet with John alone, and we would script out how I would say what I needed to say to the boys ahead of time.

At least once, each boy had a total meltdown in the car on the way to an appointment. Michael stood on the sidewalk screaming that he would not go into the office. Later Bobby did the same thing and would not move out of the car. In each instance, I called John and he came outside to meet us. He spoke quietly and calmly and didn't try to move the kid from his spot. I was amazed by him many times, and I really believe that he changed our lives with his wisdom and support.

Many times over the years, I sat in the waiting area of John's office while one or both of the boys had an appointment with him. John had a very limited magazine section which always included the latest copy of *Rolling Stone*. I picked up the March 2004 issue in May, about a year after the arrest. I thumbed through it as I sat on the tired couch in the narrow waiting room, which was crowded with toys and puzzles, since John saw mostly children in his practice. I mindlessly flipped through the magazine, sipping on iced coffee, pleased that I had once again managed to get both boys into their appointment. But I almost fell off the couch when I came across the article about the New Hampshire police officer who had arrested Jed. The detective specialized in "cyber sleuth" police work, and, according to the article, he had arrested 382 pedophiles since he began his work in 1996. The article described many of the creeps and gave excruciating details about the ways they attempted to meet their victims after starting a conversation online with the officer who was posing as a child to catch the criminal.

It was horrifying to be reading about this crap while sitting in the office of the social worker who was helping my kids recover from what their dad had done. Jed was not referenced specifically, but the article did mention how many teachers had been arrested, along with a list of other professions with the accompanying stats. It was shocking to read this national publication's piece about cybersex crimes. I felt sickened and struggled to read the entire article. It was upsetting to read about this police officer's unusual job—trolling the Internet to try to catch very sick and twisted people—because I had previously had only the utmost respect for all officers since my dad was one. In the end, I realized that I didn't have any problem with the officer, only with my ex and all the other criminals he had arrested.

Once John was done talking with the boys that day, I jumped up and said I needed to speak to him for a minute. This was very unusual, as our time was up, and the next family was already in the waiting room. John didn't hesitate at all; he saw that I was upset and gestured for me to walk in.

"Boys, sit in the waiting room. I'll be back out in a minute," I said. I pulled the magazine out of my purse, where I had stuffed it so the boys wouldn't see it.

"John, can you please throw this out? There's a huge article in here about the police officer who arrested Jed."

"Oh, I'm so sorry, Diane, I didn't know that. I'm sorry you had to see it and read it. It should not have been in my waiting room. Are you okay?"

"Yes, I'll be fine, just a little shaken up. I keep thinking we're done, and the arrest still pops up."

He threw it in his trash can right away. I don't think my boys ever saw it.

At the next appointment, I vented to John about the extensive media coverage because Jed was on the front page of the local paper again for a court appearance. I told him that every news story brought the whole event up again. He told me the boys and I were fortunate that the story was so public.

"What are you talking about? It's so embarrassing. How can this be a good thing?" I demanded. "Every news story drags the whole thing up again."

"Children suffer when they have to carry and keep secrets about their family," he responded calmly. "If kids have to keep the secret that their mom drinks too much or that Uncle Billy hits his wife, they have a huge burden to bear. Trust me, your kids are better off because the arrest is public and the community is supportive of your family in spite of it."

Having to keep our terrible situation secret would have been even more distressing for my kids than dealing with the press. Also, a strange result of the publicity of our family's situation was that other people, strangers, even, came forth and shared their secrets with me. On several occasions, someone I barely knew stopped me and poured out their heart to me, telling me things that even their loved ones didn't know. I think the media had helped to spread our story so much that people felt a kinship with us, and I was often humbled by what they shared.

One woman told me her husband who had just passed away had not died of a heart attack, as all the neighbors had been told. He had been in rehab for alcohol abuse, was discharged, and was officially homeless when his body was found at a friend's vacation home where he had crashed for a few days. He was drunk when he died. Nobody outside her immediate family knew about his battle with alcohol, and she wanted his dignity preserved, I guess, so she was sticking with the made-up story. She confided in me one day because she just had to tell someone else who had experienced lies and betrayal in a marriage.

Another time it was a male friend, an acquaintance really, who told me that he'd been hospitalized for depression although the "party line" to his coworkers had been back surgery and physical therapy.

I again felt humbled by the sharing. It seemed that the publicity of Jed's arrest had allowed people to open up to me. I hoped that I provided some consolation to these folks, and that at least they had found a sympathetic ear in me. It was a privilege when someone shared, and hopefully their burden was lifted a bit by the sharing.

With both people, we shared an important connection that lasted long after the day when they confided in me. We were soldiers in our own personal battles, but sharing and letting someone else in was a powerful coping tool. I continued to be open and honest whenever I was asked about what the boys and I had gone through, and it was always comforting to share.

My mom had kept some secrets, and I think her burden would have been lighter if she had not. After my dad died, I realized that the gender roles of my parents and their peers were very clearly defined. For example, my dad never went grocery shopping or did any cooking, unless it was grilling in the summer. My mom cleaned the house, and my dad paid the bills.

A month or so after he passed, my mom asked me to help her with the bills. It turns out she had never written a check, and she was entirely unfamiliar with the process of how to get it done. Each time we sat down to pay the bills, one or both of us would cry. We were overwhelmed with missing my dad and uncertain how to proceed without him. Their partially built dream retirement house added a whole layer of logistics and upset that we both had to deal with. Funds were tight, and his retirement payments ended with his death. Although most spouses continued to get their husband's retirement when the husband died first, that wasn't the case for my mom. We will never know why, but my dad chose his retirement package while my mom was getting chemotherapy, and he chose the plan that paid out the maximum while he was alive and ended when he died. Maybe he thought she wasn't going to live very long, but most other police officers we knew chose the plan whose payments continued after the husband died—I guess because most husbands died first. So even though my dad had been a police officer for more than thirty years, his retirement payout was small, and nothing was left for my mom. He was a kind and thoughtful man, so I don't think he made this choice with any malicious intent. It took my mom many years to wrap her head around the fact that she had to support herself. She was angry with my dad and decided not to share the news with most people we knew. She felt that it would be disloyal to my dad if she told everyone "how I was left financially."

Looking back, I realize that this caused both of us added angst— we missed him terribly, we were stressed out about money, and we couldn't tell anyone. My closest friends knew, and my mom told her two closest friends, but it took a lot of effort to be frustrated about my dad's lack of retirement benefits, to worry about finances, and to never discuss it much.

With our situation after Jed's arrest, I was always upfront about our struggles, and I learned to ask for help often. There is no doubt in my mind that this approach helped me and the boys to heal. People were so kind to us. There was no way to hide the facts because the story was in the news, and everyone knew.

Raising a child is the most difficult, laborious, committing, routine, and exhausting job one can imagine. It is a job that requires modesty, humility, presence, patience, and—most important—a great deal of maturity of character.

—Billy Moscoe-Lerman

One night the kids came home after a quick dinner with their dad. They hadn't been in the house five minutes before all hell broke loose. Initially they were arguing over who got to use the half bath first, and then they were talking over each other to tell me about their visit. I had been relaxing and watching the news but had to intervene when they began to yell and poke each other.

"Cut it out."

"Leave me alone." If you have kids, you know the drill. Things go from calm to ugly quickly when kids are cranky. Now I had to settle them so they got to sleep at a decent hour.

Whenever the boys went on visits to see their dad, it was like Russian roulette for me. I never knew what I was going to get. Sometimes one boy was excited to go and would bring a paper from school to show Jed or take along Gameboy to show him a new game. Sometimes, a boy would come back from the visit calm. More often, though, there was angst before and after the visit. The boys would be snippy with each other as they got ready to go, almost anticipating that they would be vying for their dad's attention. Afterward was almost always challenging. They would come back emotionally spent. We would argue about homework, baths, what was being served for dinner—everything. The boys would work out their frustration over their dad's situation by being miserable once they got home. It was heartbreaking to watch them try to blame anything and everything else when they were really angry at Jed.

Months rolled by. On one winter Saturday, Jed had asked if he could take the boys skiing at a small local mountain for the day. Both really wanted to go, so we had many phone conversations to plan it all out; I was nervous because it would be a much longer visit than usual.

On the morning of the ski trip, Michael woke up and announced that he didn't want to go. He was upset with his dad and wanted to stay home.

"Mom, I don't want to go skiing. Can I play with my friends today instead?" Michael asked.

"Of course, sweetie, that's fine. Bobby, are you okay going on your own with your dad?"

"I'll be fine, Mom. See you later on, Michael."

Why does this have to be so complicated? I felt bad that Michael would miss the day because he had been looking forward to it, but glad that he could speak up for himself and decide not to go. Bobby accepted that his brother decided not to ski, and went on his own with his dad. He did enjoy the day, although I'm certain he missed his brother. It was important that each boy decide when he wanted to see his dad.

One Sunday as we were walking up the steps to go into church, I was distracted and instead of thinking about church, I was running through the grocery list in my head. The rest of the day was taken up with a school project that Michael had to finish, and I needed to do a big stock-up. It seemed like we were out of everything. I was crunching the numbers in my head, working out how much was in the checking account and how much of the grocery bill would need to go on the credit card. As I got to the top of the steps, a woman named Kitty approached me. I knew her slightly from church, but we didn't know each other well because her kids went to a different elementary school. She hugged me, asked how we were doing, handed me an envelope, and walked away.

When we sat down in church, I opened up Kitty's envelope and was stunned to see a generous gift card to our local grocery store.

How had she known I was just trying to figure out how to pay for the much-needed groceries? *Wow, what a way to brighten someone's day.* On many occasions, after that first day, we would be in church on Sunday morning, and she would give me a hug and slip a gift card into my pocket. She blew me away every time because on each of the many days that she did this, we had an almost empty fridge. Her timing was uncanny. If it hadn't been for her gifts, I would have been charging groceries way more often. Grocery angel.

We never faced a situation where utilities were going to be shut off, but during the years that I was a single parent, money was something that I worried about almost daily. We lived paycheck to paycheck without much wiggle room in the budget. Twice I pulled money out of my 401K, definitely not advisable according to the investment experts, but when I did it, I felt that I didn't have any other option.

My parents and I were always into uplifting quotes. My dad used to send me mail when I was at college, and he would often enclose funny or inspiring quotes from *Reader's Digest*. Many months he clipped out the column "Laughter Is the Best Medicine" and mailed it with a letter. Sometimes it was a "Keep working hard" type of message. He would sign most letters with: "Stay busy, be happy, and remember how much we love you." I treasured his letters most when I spent a semester in London; he wrote me with news in the States, what was on TV, and what he and my mom were doing to stay busy, as he had just retired.

My mom often bought me cards with messages, especially at finals time. The bulletin board over my desk in the dorm was covered with little funny quips and meaningful messages. After the arrest, I became somewhat obsessed with inspirational quotes and had them glued to my bathroom mirror and stacked up on the vanity. First thing in the morning and last thing at night while brushing my teeth, I would read the quotes and hope to be inspired. Things like "You already have it within you" and "I know the way forward."

"Leave impressions that will bring life and cause hope in another person's soul" touched my heart.

I would need the support of those inspirational quotes as the holidays approached a year and a half after the arrest. It was my second Christmas as a single mom, and as the Christmas cards were arriving in the mail, I read one that stopped me in my tracks. The card was from a family that Jed's family had lived next to in New York when he was young. The two families had stayed in touch over the years, and the mom had addressed the card to Jed, me, and our kids and written a note that went something like this: *Hi Jed and Diane, Your boys must be getting big. We hope that you are all doing well. I wonder how your hockey team is this year, Coach Jed?*

I began to shake as I read it. Could it be that nobody in Jed's family had told this family that he'd been arrested and was awaiting sentencing? Had nobody told them that we were getting divorced and that he would never teach or coach again? I was so angry that I fired off a note to the woman and gave her the briefest of outlines of what had happened. I needed to set the record straight. I didn't think I should have to read any more cards that referred to us as married and him as a coach. She wrote back and apologized, explaining that of course they hadn't known about the arrest. I never heard from them again. It was amazing that Jed's family could live with such denial while I was working hard to clean up the mess he had made of his family.

Jed's sisters all lived out of state and would visit at the holidays. After the first year, I didn't see them or have anything to do with them when they showed up. My kids looked forward to seeing their aunts and cousins and visited without me. It always felt sad to be left at home when they went off for these visits, but I wanted my boys to enjoy their cousins. Sending them without me saved me the pain of being with the adults and having to pretend that all was wonderful in our world.

I spoke with my sister-in-law around Christmas the first year, and she warned me that their Christmas letter-card combo was on the way and said nothing about her brother's arrest. They lived far away from Massachusetts, and their neighbors didn't know about Jed's situation. Of course it would not be a good topic for the "What a great year we had" message that most people send at the holidays, but couldn't they just have not sent *us* one that year? *Why did I have to get it and open it and be reminded that, for the rest of his family, it had been a great year?*

Every Christmas, especially when the boys were small, Jed's mom had gone wild buying all of us loads of gifts. She also loved decorations and bought us many beautiful ornaments; Waterford, Lenox, and some other companies made a special ornament with the date on it, and they produced a different one each year. We had piles of them by the time the boys were eight and eleven.

After the arrest, it made me both sad and angry to unpack all our Christmas ornaments, because there were so many that she had purchased. I didn't feel like putting them on my tree, but I also couldn't get rid of them.

The second Christmas that Jed wasn't home, I bought two boxes and marked one for each of my boys. I put in all the ornaments that their grandmother had purchased, dividing them up equally. Someday when the boys had their own trees, they might like the ornaments, but now I no longer had to unpack them each December and be reminded of the way in which my relationship with my mother-in-law had ended.

When I was young, I always had a white pet rabbit. My dad built a hutch with an enclosed end so the bunny would be warm in bad weather, and it lived happily in our backyard. When I think back, I always had a bunny. I never experienced a bunny dying or picking out a new one. When I was a sophomore in college, my parents came to visit me at school. Over lunch we reminisced about my bunny because it was Easter time, and I had seen signs up at school for a bunny giveaway. That day I learned that whenever a bunny passed away, my parents would run to the local pet store and replace it. They never told me the bunny had died, because they were trying to spare me the pain, I guess. I never knew this! The best part of the story was that my dad's mom was also in the dark. She had been a frequent visitor at our house but passed away when I was small. My parents remembered that she would come to visit and remark, "That bunny got fat" or "That rabbit's ears look longer." My parents just smiled and nodded at her, apparently never letting on. Nobody wanted to tell her that it was a different bunny altogether, fearing that she might tell me. I felt silly to find out as a twenty-year-old that my parents had kept up this big ruse about my bunny throughout my childhood, but I was also touched by their kindness.

Maybe all parents struggle with when to tell their children "bad news" and when to shield them from it. I think our first reaction is to try and make everything wonderful for our kids and shelter them from difficult things. But if we don't help our kids get strong and grow resilient, we are not equipping them with the skills they need to navigate life. I was beginning to feel like an expert at delivering bad news to my kids, not a role that any mom wants. First, I had to tell them that their dad had been arrested, and now that the criminal case was finally wrapping up, there would be more bad news to share.

*The challenges before you are never greater than
the power and the love behind you.*

—Anonymous

It took two years for Jed's criminal case to be resolved. As it turns out, criminal defense attorneys usually prefer to push the final disposition of a case out as far in time from the actual event as they can. Then the defendant can hopefully demonstrate to the judge "good behavior" since the arrest. I had never practiced any aspect of criminal law, so this was news to me. It was two years, but it seemed like a lifetime had passed since the arrest. The divorce was final, and I was finishing my first year of teaching. Jed had worked with his attorneys and counselors whom they arranged to testify on his behalf.

The day before the case was to be heard, Jed came to the house to talk with the boys about the hearing and what was likely to happen. We all sat in our backyard at dinnertime, and Bobby had his baseball glove and ball in hand. He put the glove down and kept tearing at the lace on the ball as we talked. We were all nervous and upset wondering what the next day would bring. It had been a gorgeous day; the lawn needed mowing but everything was green. It seemed impossible that on another spring day we were facing a huge event, and I felt conflicted. For the boys' sake I was hoping their dad would not go to jail, but there was a huge part of me that thought he deserved it.

Jed was entering a plea of guilty, so the only uncertainty was the sentence. Possibilities ranged from a fine to incarceration. However, he had told our boys that he was quite sure he was not going to jail. His attorney was going to ask the judge for a work farm setting for punishment. This would be less restrictive than jail, and he seemed very confident about this outcome. The boys, of course, were hoping that he would not go to jail.

I, through the work of some other angels, had heard differently from some friends in law enforcement. Jed kept insisting that he wasn't going to jail. Since he didn't let me talk with his attorney, I don't know if he was in complete denial of the likelihood of jail. I have to think that his attorney gave him a reasonable summary of the facts, and he simply chose not to accept them.

I was concerned enough about his not facing reality that I wanted to do my own investigating. I needed to prepare my kids because he wasn't going to—and it was a good thing I followed that hunch. I learned from my police friends that the prosecution was pushing for jail time because of "the other kid." I was standing in the kitchen emptying the dishwasher, and the kids were asleep, when I got this information. *What other kid?* I dropped the stack of plastic bowls I was trying to put away.

I am an idiot was the first thought that went through my head. Of course there was more to the story. I didn't know about this other kid, and I should not have been listening to my ex when he said he was probably going to a work farm!

The police could provide me with only the briefest of details, but that was enough. A kid's family had come forward alleging that my ex had attempted an inappropriate relationship with him years before. The kid was in jail in another part of the country and struggling greatly with his life. The family felt that my ex was at least partly responsible for the kid's struggles and had gone to the New Hampshire district attorney when Jed's case hit the news. The way I heard it, the family did not want to prosecute, but apparently reporting the event to the DA's office was enough to impact Jed's case. The word from my friends in law enforcement was that jail time was likely.

Our police angels did two amazing things. The first was to search for the key information about what was likely to happen at the sentencing. The second was to share that information with me so I could prepare my boys. All the while their dad was telling them that he was probably going to a work farm, I knew that jail was a real possibility. John and I first met without the boys, and I filled him in on what I had learned. I left work early for the appointment, and as I was driving the short distance from school to his office, I thanked God that I had this man to help me with my boys. Sitting at a red light, I felt my stomach doing flips and once again wondered how all this crap could be happening. As soon as I walked into the waiting room, John called me in, and I blurted it all out as I dropped into the worn-out blue chair next to his.

"John, some friends in the police told me something I'm not supposed to know. It sounds like he's going to jail, but he keeps telling the kids he doesn't think he is."

"Okay, Diane, then we need to prepare the boys for the worst-case scenario."

"But I can't tell them how I learned all this. I can't talk about the police officers giving me information."

"We can talk about your work experience as a lawyer," he said.

He and I spent the rest of the appointment scripting out a conversation. I practiced it pacing in his small office, and we spoke to the boys together at our next appointment two days later. I said that based on my experience as a lawyer, I thought there was a good chance that their dad would go to jail. The kids had the same sort of stunned expressions that I had seen on their faces many times since the arrest. It must have been hard for them to understand why their dad was telling them a different story. Neither boy yelled or threw things; they just looked sad and seemed to accept what I told them. With John's help, I felt that I had prepared my boys as much as I could.

Jed never told us about the other kid.

Years after I left the school district, I learned that the principal had made Herculean efforts to protect me and the children while we were in her school. Every time Jed's story was in the paper, she emailed the entire staff—with the exception of me—and instructed them to keep the newspapers out of sight. Principal angel.

Just before the sentencing hearing, I contacted the editor of the local daily newspaper and asked him for a meeting. My plan was to ask for less coverage of Jed's hearing. Patty picked up the kids after school, and I drove right to the paper when I finished for the day. I had never been in a newspaper office, and as I sat in the waiting room, I thought about the irony of my visit. I was there to try to prevent something from getting printed. I also thought about how far I had come in the two years since Jed's arrest; I was feeling strong and hopeful about my chances for success.

As I sat in the editor's office, he asked, "What can I do for you?" I think he thought I was a salesperson or maybe I was there to ask for a charity donation from his paper. I explained who I was and who

I used to be married to. I told him I was concerned about my boys and asked if there was any way that he could keep the story of the sentencing off the front page. Initially he seemed angry that I would ask such a thing. He noted that it was an important story locally and that it would appear on the front page. He mentioned free speech and the importance of disseminating the news.

"Please hear me out. I'm not married to him anymore, he no longer lives in the area served by your paper." I took a deep breath because I could feel myself starting to shake. "But my boys and I still live here, and we are actively involved in the community."

I watched his expression change and realized I had somehow softened this curmudgeon of an editor. He looked at me and asked exactly what I wanted. This was a powerful moment for me in the saga of the arrest and its aftermath. I wanted to control the newspaper stories about the sentencing, a lofty goal. I was dreading a repeat of the type of stories we had dealt with immediately after the arrest, and I felt that if I could win this round, I would be paving a new road for me and my kids.

"Can you please stop writing that he is a former teacher? It's old news. He isn't going to return to teaching. And please don't name the town we still live in or mention that we have two boys in the school system."

"I'll see what I can do," he said.

I was thrilled and astonished by the story that appeared in print after the sentencing hearing. It bore no resemblance to the previous stories. Neither our town, the school district, nor the boys were referenced. The editor did everything that I had asked for and more. Since the arrest, I had gone from watching my friends chase the press off my front step to sitting down with the editor of the daily local paper to discuss how the story would be covered. I had become very strong and willing to tackle anything I saw as an obstacle for my family.

The day of the sentencing, we were at school. Jed told me ahead of time that his sister would call me with news of the judge's decision. It was almost the end of the school day when I finally heard from her. I had been carrying my cell phone in my pocket all day waiting for the call.

"Hi, Diane, I don't have good news," she said. "Unfortunately, he is going to jail."

"Well, he deserves it, don't you think?" I barked at her. I don't remember much of the rest of the conversation, but I'm sure I was abrupt with her. She sounded upset, but I had nothing to offer her in the way of consolation.

Now I had to tell my kids.

I left school earlier than usual; I dreaded giving the boys the news, but I couldn't put it off. As soon as the three of us were home, the kids wanted to know what had happened. *How am I going to break this news to them?* As we sat in the family room on the couch, I held in my tears and told them that their dad was going to jail for at least eighteen months, not to the work farm that he had hoped for. None of us actually cried, but we were all very close to tears. We sat together for a while, hugging each other. It had taken a long two years, but we finally had a conclusion of sorts. I realized that my day-to-day life was not going to change much, as I still needed to work and take care of my kids.

Our greenhouse was one of my favorite places as a child. My dad had built an addition to our house which you could walk into from the backyard. You could also get to it from a set of wooden steps which led down to the stone floor of the greenhouse from our den. Every once in a while, my dad would say, "Come out to the greenhouse, Dianey, so I can show you what's blooming." I would sit on the top step, and my dad would explain everything. I loved the Christmas cactus plants and admired their adherence to a schedule. They knew exactly when to start showing their brilliant pink and red blossoms in order to be ready for Christmas. Dad would start his seeds for the vegetable garden in late winter, and the two large shelves he had built were full of different plants all year. The greenhouse was often humid, especially after he had watered everything; the glass walls and ceiling creating the perfect "hothouse" for his hobby. The smell of the damp soil would linger long after the watering was done. Even now when I am in a humid greenhouse, it brings me back to sitting on those wooden steps talking to my dad. I knew, growing up, that my dad not only expected great things from me but that he also believed I could accomplish them. It was hard to impress him, but I always tried to do just that. He helped me to be strong and to feel confident, and I hoped to instill the same things in my sons.

My dad took me to the Franklin Park Zoo many times over the years, and we passed right by it whenever we drove to Haymarket for meat and produce. The zoo was, and still is, located in a "tough" area, but I always felt safe with my dad. Our car displayed his police sticker, and his badge was tucked into the pocket of his civilian clothes whenever we were out and about.

There was a part of me that hoped Jed's incarceration would be difficult and dangerous. I thought he deserved to suffer in light of what he had done. At the same time, though, I didn't want my boys to have a father in jail—what a terrible burden to manage. I hoped that I could give my kids the strength they would need, the same strength that I had been blessed to receive from my dad.

My mom often said after Jed's arrest that maybe it was a good thing my dad had passed away. If he had been alive to witness his arrest and the resulting difficulties for us, he might have taken the law into his own hands to protect me and my kids. I never saw my dad do anything scary or harmful to another individual, but I had to agree with her. He might have hurt Jed if he had been alive to see it all go down.

Forced busing began in Boston in 1974 when I was entering seventh grade. A federal judge had determined that the schools were not equal, and to make things fair, he ordered that students be bused out of their neighborhoods to attend school in other parts of the city. Many residents of the city were up in arms. White families didn't want their kids going to school in black neighborhoods, and black families didn't want their kids going to schools in white neighborhoods.

That was my first year at Boston Latin School, the oldest public school in the country. Because it was an exam school, I was unaffected by the busing. Directly across the street from Latin was Boston English High School. Due to the tension in the city, we started the first few weeks of school with Tactical Patrol Force officers in full riot gear lined up and down both sides of the street. They stood three feet apart and were menacing to look at—a scary way to start school. Those officers stood at attention all day.

All Boston police officers, including my dad, had to work a lot of overtime that fall. In almost every neighborhood, there were daily protests. Parents stood on street corners throwing things at buses full of students with a different skin color than their own. It was a scary time in Boston. My mom was distraught worrying about my dad working these near riots and me at a new school with police lined up on the street all day. But our family was lucky; we got through the crisis in the city unscathed. My mom and I both felt safe knowing that my dad was watching over us and the city.

I tried hard to protect my sons as we dealt with Jed's arrest and all the events that followed. I had learned from my dad the importance of being a protector, never imagining that I would have to raise my kids alone and guide them through a horrible situation.

When I was a young girl, my mom often had some sort of craft lined up for me on a weekend afternoon. Over the years she taught me to sew, embroider, knit, and crochet. She was not a big fan of my watching lots of television, preferring to teach me things instead. At Christmastime, she would set up the basement for "projects," and I'd have my neighborhood friends over to make wreaths or decorate small trees. I think her focus was twofold: for us to learn something new and to make a gift for someone. She always said that a gift we made was more special than something we bought.

Now, she did the same thing for my boys. She enjoyed setting up activities for them. Each year, they colored Easter eggs. Mom would boil lots of eggs and set up bowls with a different tint of food coloring in each one. She put out placemats and spoons, and my kids had a ball sloshing the eggs around in the bowls of color. Later on when the eggs cooled, round two consisted of decorating the eggs with magic markers or gluing on glitter. Doing eggs with my mom, making duct tape wallets, and building bookcases from kits helped my boys take their minds off their distress about their dad.

Everything I know I learned from dogs.

—Nora Roberts, American author

Like many little boys, my sons really wanted a dog. They often asked for one, and their pleas became more frequent around the time of the sentencing. Michael had researched breeds, and both boys promised that they would do the walking, the feeding, and all things dog-related if I assented. I called Maria late one night and asked her, "Should I get the boys a dog? I think their dad is going to jail. Would a dog help ease the blow?"

"Of course, get the dog," she said.

And just like that, I caved in; I couldn't deny their request. I had never owned a dog and was concerned about the longer "to do list" that a new puppy would bring, but I felt so bad for them because of their dad. The boys had discovered that a Cairn terrier caused fewer allergy issues than most dogs, and this was important because of my mom's allergies. We also liked the idea of a small dog, and a Cairn was the perfect size for us. We found a breeder out of state and made our choice, a wheat-colored female. She looked just like Toto from *The Wizard of Oz* except that she was tan and brown instead of black.

After school one day, Bobby and I drove to the airport to pick up our dog, who was being transported to us from the South. We were so excited on the car ride into the city. Michael was on a band field trip that day and was disappointed that he was going to miss the arrival. We had to promise that we would bring the dog with us when we picked him up from the field trip. He said he wouldn't be able to wait until we got home to see our new family member.

When Bobby and I got to the airport, we went to the baggage claim and asked where we could find our dog. We were directed through a maze of corridors and finally to a small office behind baggage. This is truly the back of the airport and a place that you would never see as a passenger. Bobby was excited, bouncing in place while I showed our paperwork.

The little old guy behind the counter read the papers and looked right at my boy, totally ignoring me. "You picking up a new dog, young man?"

Bobby beamed. "Yes, is our dog here?"

"Wait one second and I'll be right back."

It seemed like forever, but our friendly airport worker was back in a minute or two. He handed us a small, maroon crate. We were delighted to see a furry little face peeking out at us behind the grill in the front. Bobby opened the crate and squealed with delight when he picked up our tiny Cairn terrier for the first time. He put a leash on the dog, and we started to head out of the terminal.

"Have fun," the man behind the counter yelled to us as we waved to him. The floors of the terminal were so slippery that our little dog couldn't walk very well, making us laugh as she tried hard to keep up with us. Bobby quickly decided to pick her up and carry her instead. I took the crate, and we made our way to the parking garage. It took us a few minutes to load the crate and get settled in for the ride. My passengers enjoyed getting to know each other as we drove home; I kept glancing in the rearview mirror as I fought traffic, and the scene melted my heart.

As soon as we got home, three of the neighborhood kids rang the doorbell, wanting to see the new dog that they knew was arriving that day. Bobby ran to the door, and before I could get to him, I heard him say, "You guys can't meet the dog yet. My brother has to meet her first!" He slammed the door in their faces and ran back in to the kitchen to be with the dog. I was annoyed with him for being rude to the kids, but I was so touched by his loyalty to his brother. There was no reprimand that seemed appropriate.

Fortunately, we had only an hour before it was time to pick up Michael at school. By the time we arrived, there were several families waiting for the busload of students to return. It was a warm spring night, and parents and kids stood chatting in the parking lot, enjoying the weather. As soon as I pulled up, people came over to us, since the boys had apparently told everyone the exciting news, and their buddies were eager to see our new addition. One dad asked me if it was okay to stand next to us. "I'd like to be here to see Michael's face when he sees the dog for the first time," he said. I understood. It was such a happy moment for our family, and it was sweet of this guy to want to witness it.

Before long, the bus pulled in, and Michael practically leaped off it. He raced over to us, followed by his buddies in the band, shouting, "Come on, guys, let's go see my new dog!"

Pretty soon the puppy was surrounded by her two new boys, a bunch of sweaty middle schoolers, their instruments and backpacks dropped on the pavement, and their parents. Quite a welcoming committee! Michael told us that all day he was wondering what the dog would look like. He couldn't wait for the field trip to be over so he could meet her. I will always remember that ride home from school, our first night home with our little dog, and how happy and proud my boys were. The dog's tail seemed to wag nonstop, so she was happy too. We named her Keiara after one of the characters in *The Lion King*, one of our all-time favorite movies.

Good move, Mom, I thought, *letting yourself get talked into the dog.*

That summer we were a common fixture in the neighborhood. The boys and I would grab the dog, put her on her leash, and go for a stroll around the block. We were proud and happy to be new dog owners, so we enjoyed having people stop and ask questions about her. One hot day, before we got too far from our house, we began to worry about the dog. It had been a hot summer, and we were afraid the small terrier would overheat.

"Mom, Keiara looks hot, and she's walking slow and panting," Bobby said.

"I don't think she can walk anymore," Michael announced. "We should carry her."

Soon I was holding the leash as the boys took turns carrying the dog. Our neighbors teased us that we weren't giving the dog enough exercise when they saw us rounding the corner.

We were so overprotective of our newest family member that our summer walks turned into "carries." When the boys did their summer reading assignments, they preferred the kitchen-family room rather than their upstairs bedrooms. Whenever possible, they worked on the couch, and the dog would always snuggle in, sometimes getting in the way as they tried to write. Michael often said, "Keiara is the only one in the family who likes homework." The longer the assignment, the more cuddle time she got.

One night about a year after we got the dog, we had her out on her run just before bed for the final "pee break" of the day and suddenly she began to bark and whine. We knew from the sound that something was wrong, and as soon as we walked outside, we could smell it—a skunk had been by to visit. As we got closer to Keiara, we saw her rubbing her face. The poor thing had been sprayed and the whole yard smelled awful. We brought her inside, the three of us fighting back tears. We felt bad but didn't know what to do for her.

The boys went back and forth between, "Mom, what are we going to do?" and, "Yuck, this smells awful!" We were still amateur dog owners without any experience to draw on, but I remembered hearing somewhere that V8 could take the smell away. We had a can of tomato juice in the kitchen, so we wrestled the dog into the bathtub and tried to cover her with the soupy red juice. She wasn't too happy with us, and by the time we were done, the three of us had more juice on us than the dog. We had become very attached to Keiara, and I felt like I had let her down somehow in letting her get sprayed.

It was late, and I was worried about us getting up for school the next day, so we put the dog in her crate, went to bed, and brought her to the vet the following afternoon. The vet's treatment was more effective than ours by far, but not cheap. I paid with a credit card and thought, *I'll worry about this bill later*. It took a while for the smell to dissipate from the house, but we were proud of ourselves for the way we took care of our little dog in our first big crisis as dog owners. We had worked together and figured out what needed to be done.

After that, we stayed with her on the lawn when we brought her out at night so we could stand guard and protect her from neighborhood skunks.

It just ain't possible to explain some things. It's interesting to wonder on them and do some speculations, but the main thing is you have to accept it—take it for what it is, and get on with your growing.

—Jim Dodge

Over the years, when I was frustrated in my dealings with my ex-husband, I would often vent to the kids' counselor. "He keeps disappointing them, making plans without asking me first," I would say, or "I worry that he will say things to them about his life that are inappropriate." John freed me up when he said, "Concentrate on establishing a good relationship with your boys. You can't control their father's relationship with them."

This helped me immensely. I still got upset with my ex's behavior, but I had learned that I could not control it.

During the time that he was incarcerated, Jed often wrote the boys long letters, sometimes more than a dozen pages. Occasionally they wrote back. Michael and I had an argument one night because he wanted help with the correct address for a letter to his dad.

"Mom, what's Dad's address?" he asked innocently.

I barked at him, "I don't know how to address a letter to a jail—the address is weird." I slammed the kitchen cabinet as I took out the dishes for dinner.

"Just a minute, let me look." The poor kid—while I searched for the tiny scrap of paper I had written Jed's address on, I slammed more of the drawers and cabinets. *Why does he need to send him a letter? I don't want him to send a letter. Jed does not deserve a letter.* I was ranting, I was angry and annoyed, and I needed to get dinner on the table. After checking the bulletin board, looking through my address book, and slamming the last few drawers for emphasis, I finally calmed down. Michael was understandably upset with me for my tirade and stomped upstairs to his room.

I finally found the address, called up to Michael, and gave it to him so he could mail the letter. I also apologized to my boy for snapping at him. We were both upset about so many things, and the address had just been a trigger. I wanted Jed to suffer; I didn't want him to get mail, I didn't want Michael to write to his father in jail—the whole situation was ridiculous. I felt bad for taking it out on my kid.

Jed wrote to the boys about TV shows, movies, and sporting events that he had watched. *There's TV in jail? Doesn't sound too tough.*

Sometimes there were scores and play-by-play summaries from a Red Sox game that he had been able to see. Why would the kids want to read that a week after the game? He also included elaborate drawings of things that he thought they would like, so they got Hogwarts, Hedwig, and Fenway, usually in many different colors. One time he drew an elaborate picture of the front of the house, one he had to have drawn from memory. It was eerie because it was so accurate and detailed. I opened one letter and began to sob. The stupid drawing felt like a knife in my chest. How long must this picture have taken to draw? Two hours? Four hours? I always read everything first because I worried about what he might say and whether it was appropriate. The content was usually fine, but it bothered me to have to read all his nonsense.

While he drew and drew and drew, I worked, folded baskets of laundry, vacuumed the house, cooked, cleaned up from dinner, helped with homework, negotiated showers with two boys who insisted they did not need them, did my grad school homework, emptied the dishwasher, readied the lunchboxes and breakfast dishes for the next day, and collapsed into bed. Those drawings were maddening. *How could he have nothing to do but color all day? What kind of sentence was it to sit and draw? Isn't jail supposed to be a punishment?*

At first when the letters came, the boys were eager to read them. Over time, they became less enthralled. Michael or Bobby would grab the mail when we got home, take a quick look at the artwork, skim the letter, and then ask if they could run outside to play. The letters seemed to lose their intrigue during his time in jail.

It looked like Jed was taking art classes, based on the number of drawings that were mailed to the boys each week. I'm sure he was thoughtfully creating things he thought the boys would like, and I'm sure he hoped that the pictures would help him maintain a connection with our boys while he was away. But at that time when every day was so challenging for us, those pictures really ticked me off. I resented the free time he had and thought he should be digging ditches instead.

One day one of my teacher colleagues asked me how things were going as we stood in the hallway in between classes. She taught geography, and she was the most youthful grandma I had ever met. She always wore bright colors with matching giant earrings, and I loved being in her classroom each day.

"We're doing okay. I'm grateful to be on my boys' school schedule, and I really like teaching."

"Forgive me for intruding, but I need to ask you—did you have a wonderful childhood? Your parents must have raised you well and given you the strength that you needed to survive Jed's arrest and take care of your boys." She complimented me on how well I was doing. I was blown away—what a fabulous concept, to have somebody decide that I was put together well enough to handle this mess! I thought of her kind statement many times afterward. It empowered me on tough days when I was far from certain I was doing a good job.

Mostly I was filled with doubt and worry. In addition to the emotional trauma of the arrest and the divorce, there were many "guy" things that I didn't know how to do, and thankfully we had a lot of help. When the boys were invited to bar mitzvahs and needed to wear a tie, I realized that I had no idea how to tie one. I sent them next door to our kind neighbor who tied it properly. When both kids were in Scouts and we had to make a Pinewood Derby car, I was lost. My colleague at the middle school who taught shop helped us out after school several years in a row. It really does take a village to help a mom raise two boys. I was good at making brownies and organizing playdates, but I knew that my skill set only went so far.

After Jed had been in jail for a year, he started asking the boys to visit him when he spoke to them during their weekly phone call. They were now eleven and fourteen. It made me crazy that he would ask them, because clearly they could not drive themselves. I knew that he hoped to generate enthusiasm for the idea of a family jail visit by bringing it up with the boys first.

After lots of conversations back and forth, a Saturday in the fall was selected as visitation day. Of course, I was dreading the whole thing, but the boys definitely wanted to see their dad. I worried about how harsh the jail would be and pictured dirt and squalor and scummy people. I feared that the visit to the jail would only traumatize my kids, and I wanted to spare them that. They'd had only letters and phone calls over the first year of the sentence. I did not want to go, and I did not want my precious boys in a jail, but I had to be there to support them. I was raising my boys to be gentlemen and to have class and dignity. Visiting their father in jail was exactly the opposite of the type of life experience that I hoped to give them.

The amazing group of friends who had supported us every day since the arrest stepped up again on the planning for the jail visit. Many friends offered to handle the ninety-minute drive and others offered to host us for dinner when we got back. After lots of discussion, the kids and I decided that Jon would drive us and we would go to Maria's house afterward.

On the ride up to New Hampshire, I remember looking at the beautiful New England foliage and thinking with envy of the tourists we were sharing the highway with. I was jealous of everyone who did not have to go to jail that day. I was angry at Jed for asking this of us. The drive passed quickly, and before I knew it, we were pulling into the parking area.

When the visit was in the planning stages, I had tried hard to talk the boys out of going. "Are you sure you want to do this?" I asked. "It might be awful inside, and it's probably going to be upsetting." I kept hoping that they wouldn't want to go—but no such luck. The boys kept talking over each other and saying nervously, "Look, Mom, it's fine." We stood next to Jon's car as we stared at the buildings in front of us.

I don't know what I was expecting, but all we saw were concrete blocks rising up high. There was nothing menacing on the outside. The only startling sight was the roll of barbed wire at the top of the blocks, extending as far as you could see. The fact that the sun was out and the sky was blue made the whole view of the building less scary than I had been picturing in my mind in the weeks leading up to the visit.

We piled out of the car and trudged up to the visitors' entrance. Jon was going to wait for us outside. The next step was walking through the metal detector and giving our names to the corrections officer. Then we had to wait on wooden benches that were lined up against the wall. It was early October, but many of the children around us waiting to go in were wearing Halloween costumes. The action heroes and the little fairies looked so out of place in the dingy hallway. The costumes were supposed to be cheery, but I felt so sad when I looked at the kids. The glitter that rubbed off the fairy wings barely showed up on the dirty, well-worn floor.

After a brief wait, our name was called, and we were escorted into the visiting area. We were told to stay in our seats until Jed was brought in. I felt so nervous as we waited, but I was far more angry. How could he have done this to us? Why did we have to sit in this awful place to wait and see him for thirty minutes? My boys deserved so much better.

When I looked up, Jed was walking toward us in his bright

orange jumpsuit. I should have realized he'd be wearing orange, but I hadn't thought about it and it took me by surprise. He was thin but otherwise looked unremarkable. There were old board games piled in the corner of the room, their boxes tattered and dusty. The guard told us that our two choices of activities were to play games or to buy snacks from the vending machine. We opted for snacks because the games looked so tired. While Jed remained in his seat, the three of us went to the vending machine; I wanted the boys to be right next to me. My hands shook as I tried to fit the coins in the slot. *Really, how can we be here today? How did it come to be that I am at a jail with my precious children? I can't wait to get us out of here.*

We brought the snacks back to the very wobbly table. Jed tried to keep the boys talking about school and their other activities, but there were many awkward pauses. The boys and I were distracted and nervous, and we kept glancing around the room and studying everyone else. The room was jammed with tables, and at each one there was a man in orange. Each man had broken a family with his stupidity, and I wanted to scream at all of them.

Finally there was an announcement from the guard. "That's it, visiting is done," he yelled. And then, blessed relief, time was up. I was thrilled, but my last worry was that either the boys or Jed would get upset when we left.

Touching was not allowed, so after Jed sort of waved to the boys as he walked out, the officer unlocked the door and let us back out into the hallway. I was relieved that the parting was uneventful. Both boys looked at the ground as we left; they looked sad, and we all walked slowly and without speaking. What would I have done if Jed had fallen apart or the kids had melted down? In retrospect, it went well. If any jail visit can be described as smooth and uneventful, this was it.

The three of us were exhausted by the event and quiet for the long ride home. Both boys stared out of the window and were unusually quiet. Jon didn't try to encourage conversation; he just drove and sipped his coffee.

By the time we got to Maria's house at dinnertime, we were hungry and happy for the company of her family. She fed us well, and being there was the perfect antidote for our terrible trip.

A few months later, Michael went online when I wasn't home and read everything that he could find about his father's arrest. He announced when I came in the door, "I read it all, Mom. I know you didn't want me to, but I needed to know."

I was unsure how to react. Part of me was relieved that he knew, but I worried about the content of some of the emails his father had written and about the news articles—there were so many and they were explicit.

I called Maria, and she came right over to help field Michael's questions and the storm of emotion I thought would follow. Michael was upset at first about the things he was finding out, but he understood, in the end, that I had protected him because he was so young. Maria offered to go for a walk with him, and he readily agreed. She wisely thought he might be more comfortable talking about some of the sexual parts without his mother being there. I prayed as they walked out the door, *Please watch over my boy and give him strength to deal with this news.*

She told me later that their conversation was intense, and my boy's questions had shown his maturity.

Michael didn't end up tossing furniture or punching walls, but he decided that he wasn't going to speak to or see his dad. That lasted for two years. Jed was sad but knew that he had no bargaining power. Later, when Jed was released, he visited with Bobby and he sent Michael greeting cards and gifts on holidays, usually writing things like, "I miss you and hope that one day soon we can visit again."

Within the first few years after the initial diagnosis, I had several MS relapses. About a year after being diagnosed, I lost the hearing in my left ear. I didn't think about the MS, and I went straight to an ear, nose, and throat doctor.

He struggled to diagnose me until at the end of the appointment I mentioned MS. He was very kind and did not try to mask his relief. He admitted that he initially thought I had a brain tumor (familiar pattern here!) but was now fairly sure this issue was MS-related. As I stared at the diplomas on the wall of his small examining room, I was sweating and nervous. I prayed that I would be able to tolerate the steroids and that they would work. It was scary not to hear anything at all on my left side.

My neurologist prescribed IV steroids administered over five days at the hospital as an outpatient and then ten days of pills at home. Fortunately, my hearing came back completely before the course of steroids was completed.

The "steroid rage" was hard to tolerate. I would be up all night, unable to sleep and jittery from the meds. I also was short-tempered and bitchy. Turns out that 'roid rage is really a thing! But I was happy to put up with the steroids since they worked so well. Then began a roller coaster of uncertainty; each time I felt a twinge or a weird symptom I wondered if I should go to the neurologist.

Everything from a headache to a cold had me worried that I would need steroids again. By the time I experienced the second flare-up, about a year after the first, I knew what it was and knew that I needed the steroids. The symptoms got worse over a couple of days; I lost the use of my right hand again. I couldn't hold a pen, and I had to write with my left hand. Another time I exercised too much and both of my legs felt like "pins and needles" constantly. I couldn't feel my feet and was afraid that I would fall. The MRI revealed a new lesion on my thoracic spine, and steroids were prescribed once again.

We never went back to visit Jed in jail. Throughout the next year, he often asked the kids to visit him; at one point, we even had the second visit scheduled. But on the morning that we were supposed to go, both boys suddenly told me that they felt "sick." Stomachaches had appeared out of nowhere, but I was confident that my boys were actually quite healthy. They were telling me they didn't want to go back to jail, but I understood they couldn't say it out loud. I guess they felt loyal enough to their dad that feigning stomachaches was easier. I told the boys that we wouldn't reschedule the visit, and I think they were relieved.

As there was no way to notify Jed that we were not coming, I guess he sat there waiting for the escort to the visiting area, but the escort never showed up. Several days later when he was able to call us, he was almost frantic that we had not visited, wondering what had gone wrong. I got on the phone and said there were not going to be any more visits.

"Listen, the boys said they felt sick on the day we were supposed to visit you. I don't think they were really sick. I think they were so upset last time that they didn't want to go again. Could you do me a favor and stop asking the boys when they will visit you?" One trip there had been enough. He was quiet, and I know he was very disappointed by this request, but to his credit, he didn't badger the kids about another visit but seemed to accept what I had told him.

I compare everything to The Day We Visited Him in Jail. Nothing afterward was anywhere near as challenging as that day had been.

I can overcome hopelessness.

—Anonymous

Three years after my diagnosis, my neurologist recommended a new medication. I was happy because I would have only three injections each week with the new one, not seven. She thought this was the right time to change meds since I had experienced several relapses on the prior one. I was scared to switch, but I was—and still am—very fond of my doctor, and I have confidence in her, so after reading up on her recommendation, I agreed to the change.

The new medication had several potential side effects, including flu-like symptoms. Those side effects hit hard. After injecting, I would often wake up with chills that were so severe I was practically bouncing off the bed. When I stopped freezing, the sweats would sometimes set in. Often in the mornings after injecting, I still felt queasy and would have ginger ale and saltines for breakfast. Fortunately, I did not experience the side effects with every dose, but the day after a tough night was a long one. The lack of sleep and the nausea would make me cranky, resulting in a challenging teaching and mothering day.

None of this was fun, but since the medication seemed to be working, it was definitely worth putting up with the occasional night of side effects. Neurologists measure the success of a medication by the number of new lesions that show up on MRI. No new lesions is the best news an MS patient can get.

Around this time, I decided I was ready to start dating. It wasn't a sudden idea but had grown slowly over time. I spent time with my friends and their families, none of whom were divorced. I still believed in "couples" and felt that we were meant to have another half to share life with. I wanted to live my life, even if MS made me tired, and even if the meds left me feeling crappy sometimes.

Although I was committed to being honest with my children about everything, I made an exception when I had a blind date. I had actually discussed this with their social worker, and we agreed that it wasn't appropriate to share my dates with my kids. I told the boys that I had a meeting for a class, or I would arrange playdates for them while I went out. This was fairly easy to do since I did not have many dates. It made going out more complicated, but my friends were always happy to host them—it gave them first dibs on the date details!

My first date was in June of 2006. An old boyfriend from high school had looked me up and asked me out for coffee. I was so nervous as I drove to meet him at a local Panera, because I worried that I would not recognize him. Would it be awkward to chat after not seeing each other in so many years? I wracked my brain to try to remember what I had heard about his life. Did he have two kids or three? Was he still into computers or was that old news? We had exchanged a couple of brief emails before meeting in person, and I realized how little information I actually had.

The closer I got to Panera, the more of a wreck I was. It seemed like a big moment, my first date as a "mature mom." I pulled into the parking lot and checked my hair in the rearview mirror. Then I jumped as I opened the car door because my date was standing there. He must have been sitting in his car waiting for me to drive in.

We had a pleasant chat over coffee, but as I was getting ready to leave, he let me know that he wanted to start dating me right away and often. He claimed he had been thinking of me often over the years, and now that he was divorced, he was eager for us to "try again" even though it had been many years since our high school romance. Yikes! I was flattered but not interested in dating him. I had viewed this first date as a practice run for me, and I was grateful to him for reaching out. His interest gave me confidence as I ventured into the dating pool. He was very persistent and kept calling me, even though I turned down his many invitations. Eventually he got the message, and I do hope he is well and happy.

I felt like a high school kid when I started dating. I was nervous but also hopeful—maybe there was still a good guy out there who was single.

A male friend said, "I'm surprised you would ever want to go on a date after what Jed did to you."

"Not all men are liars and cheats," I said.

There had to be some good ones out there still. Every one of my friends was still married to their first spouse. By all accounts the institution of marriage seemed to be thriving for most people; my horrible divorce certainly wasn't the norm.

I was reluctant to use the dating websites that were just getting popular, because anything computer-related turned my stomach. I figured I would tell everyone I knew that I was ready to date, and friends of friends seemed better than dating total strangers.

My neighbor Chris told me about a guy, and I met Greg at a bar for a quick drink one night. We had fun for forty minutes, which was a good return to the dating world, and when he called me for a second date, I agreed. I was shocked when I met him at the hostess stand for date number two. He was a foot shorter than me, maybe more. I realized that on our first date he had been seated at the bar before I arrived and when I left—I did not know his height! No way could I date someone that much shorter than me. He was nice, but it was too weird.

Next up was my friend Martha, who knew a guy just wrapping up his second marriage—that was a red flag for me, but I had said I wanted to date, so I didn't want to turn Martha down since she was nice enough to help me out. I spoke to Ted on the phone, and we agreed to meet at a restaurant near me a few nights later. We gave each other brief descriptions: "I will meet you near the front entrance," I said. "I have short brown hair and I'm about five foot six."

He replied, "I have gray hair and glasses."

I was about to hang up the phone when he added, "I will be wearing a red scarf so you can find me." I'm sure he thought this was helpful, but I cracked up—why would he need to add the part about the scarf? How many guys with gray hair and glasses would be waiting by the front door of the small restaurant we had agreed to meet at? I met him for the date, and I couldn't get over the fact that he was actually wearing a bright red, long wool scarf. I couldn't wait for the meal to end. He was nice but still stuck on his soon-to-be ex-wife.

My friends were concerned about my getting hurt, so they watched me like a hawk. It was not uncommon for my phone to buzz three times on a date—Marylee, Maria, or Trish checking in to see if I was alright. I "used" a call from Marylee only once when I wanted to end a date early. I was pretty sure that the night was going to end awkwardly because Jim was hinting about my going to his apartment, and I had no interest in that. Leaving dinner early to go take care of my "sick kid" gave me an out when my phone rang.

Date number four taught me a lot about what not to say. He was a nice guy by the name of Dave who had been widowed the year before. He shared the details of his wife's illness and his care for her. It was very touching, and he certainly seemed like a compassionate, caring guy. Halfway through dinner, he asked why I got divorced. Because he had told me so much about his wife's illness, I blurted out the details of the attempted solicitation and arrest. Bad move. I watched his face fall and thought, *I will never hear from this guy. He is horrified by the story of my divorce.* I had just learned something important: never tell the story on a first date. Before I told someone the saga of my first marriage, they needed to know me first.

Shortly after that date, Mary and Chuck set me up with Doug. I was standing at the hostess desk of the restaurant we had agreed to meet at, feeling awkward and nervous. *Why am I doing this? I am too old for dating.* I looked up as the door opened and a guy walked in. I thought, *That guy is so cute. I won't be that lucky—that won't be him.* He quickly walked right by me and into the restaurant so I figured he was meeting a group of people. *Damn!* Two minutes later he came back out. "Are you Diane? I'm Doug."

Oh happy day—he was my date! He was tall and gorgeous.

Halfway through our meal, my stomach hurt from laughing. He was funny and self-deprecating. I liked the shirt he was wearing, and when I complimented him on it, he joked about it being the only clean one he had. He ran his own business and we had a long conversation about workers' compensation insurance. I was struck by his intelligence and his work ethic. For a guy who was so accomplished and so smart, he was not arrogant or impressed with himself. His humility was charming.

Then came the Big question – why I divorced. I mumbled the speech that I had been practicing in the bathroom mirror: "It's not a great first date story, trust me." My refusal to tell him piqued his curiosity—he really wanted to know!

"You can tell me. My ex struggled, and our divorce was really nasty," he kindly offered. I was sorely tempted to tell all but kept my guard up and refused to spill the beans about Jed, even though he gently pressed me for details.

There was a table of about a dozen senior citizens next to us, and throughout the meal Doug and I commented on them because they seemed to be having a great time. "What kind of group do you think it is?" I asked him. We kept speculating, maybe a church choir, maybe a college reunion. They were all around the same age, and some were couples but not all.

As we left the restaurant, we walked over to them. We hadn't discussed it in advance, but we both stopped to ask what brought them together. They replied that the ladies had gone to nursery school together and had stayed friends over the years, getting together with their spouses. We were both touched. I felt a connection with Doug because of the encounter, as I knew that he shared my curiosity about the world and people.

When we walked outside, we exchanged phone numbers and agreed to get in touch.

I floated home; I liked him so much. I was distracted with thoughts of Doug and romance, which seemed silly since it was August, and the boys and I were busy getting ready to go back to school. I didn't really have time to date, and what was I thinking? I have kids to take care of—dating is a silly idea, isn't it? Edith and I had lunch on Monday, two days after I met Doug. We acted like teenage girls giggling over my date and speculating when he might call. She asked me to tell her all about him and sat patiently while I droned on and on. She predicted that he would call midweek. I thought he might call the following week, but I hoped I was wrong. I wanted him to call in time to set up a date for the weekend. She asked me what I had worn on the first date, and we planned out what I should wear if we went out again, discussing different options depending on where we might go. I ran through my whole wardrobe, and we decided that I would either go with my white capris and a black tank or the pink sundress I had just bought at Marshall's. Since Doug is tall, I could wear my favorite sandals with heels—not an option with short guys! I was excited to think that I had met someone I actually liked and wanted to see again. I didn't think about Jed at all, as my marriage to him seemed like a distant memory. I now thought of my family as the boys and me.

Two long days after my lunch with Edith, Doug called me to ask about another date. It was amazing that I didn't wear out the phone checking to see if anyone was trying to reach me—I was so eager for his call.

On date number two, we met at a local river at noon, bought sandwiches, and sat on a bench on a beautiful late August day. He told me about the jobsite he was working on, and I told him the details of getting my classroom ready for my students. Since I had come right from school, I was wearing shorts and sneakers. He was in work clothes too. So much for all my outfit planning with Edith. At the end of the hour, we stood up from the bench and gathered our trash for the barrel. I was nervous but I also didn't want our date to end. We dumped our trash, and then he leaned over to pull me into a hug; he kissed me and then, while still holding me, said, "So is it okay for you tell me now about your divorce? It's our second date, not our first."

Deep breath, Di. Okay, let it rip and see what happens. I like him and if he can't stand this story, it's better to know now.

After I told him about the arrest, the jail sentence, and being a single mom, he said, "Hmm, that's awful. I never heard about that. Do you want to go out again?"

I was torn between feeling incredulous that he claimed not to have heard the story and excited that he wanted to go on date number three.

Later on, he admitted that, of course, he had heard about the story—you'd have to be under a rock to miss the extensive news coverage. But I was thrilled with his acceptance and nonchalant attitude toward my messy history.

"Hey, Di, I think I'm going to go out and buy two thank-you cards, one for your ex-husband and one for my ex-wife." I cried when he said it, because it was the most romantic thing anyone had ever said to me. There was a country song that brought me to tears the first time I heard it, something about a cracked road bringing two people together. It summed up our lives so well, because we weren't starting out as young loves. We had both lived a lot before we met, and we had both endured hardship and sadness as a result of our divorces. Doug and I traded stories about being broke, charging groceries because there wasn't enough cash, being in counseling to deal with divorce, and keeping the heat low in the house to make ends meet after our marriages broke up.

Our children (a total of five) had experienced sadness and had struggled because of their parents' divorces. A new love in our forties was a cause for celebration.

In March 2007, the New England late winter reared its ugly head. Bobby had strep and was home from school. I was taking care of him when I went outside to get the mail and noticed that ice dams were backing up the water and sending it into the house. I began to shovel the ice, and in between rounds of chipping ice, I ran in to check on my patient. Doug called me to check in. "How is everything over there?"

As soon as I heard his voice, I dissolved into tears. "I've been out there all morning shoveling, but I can't stop the flow of water." As I was telling the story, I was crying; I was overwhelmed and didn't know what to do. He arrived at my house within an hour and helped me chip away at the ice. As soon as I saw his truck pull up, I knew the house would be fine and the ice would be gone. Doug even climbed up onto the roof and shoveled off some wintery mix as well. How amazing it was to have a teammate and a helper that day.

Some of my happiest childhood memories are when my dad would take me on an adventure. We often went to Jamaica Pond or Larz Anderson to feed the ducks. We would buy a new loaf of white bread, something we never ate at home. I would feed the ducks and enjoy eating a slice or two myself, rolling the white part of the bread into squishy balls. It's much easier to throw balls of bread than slices of bread! On Saturday mornings, we often went to Haymarket in Boston to buy fresh produce from the pushcarts. We also went to the meat market, located in what is now a tourist attraction, Quincy Market. I found the meat market a little scary as a kid, but I loved being with my dad. To get to the meat shops, which were below street level, you had to walk down a set of stone steps. The steps were old and worn with indentations in the middle, probably from years of use. When I was very young, my dad took my hand on the steep steps. The butchers behind the counter wore white aprons that were never white but were covered in blood. Giant slabs of beef and pork hung from hooks in the ceiling. They were scary to look at. While my dad placed our order, the man in charge always leaned over the counter to hand me a slice of salami, which I loved. I didn't like standing too close to the big glass cases, because looking at the raw meat made me queasy. All the meat stalls had a strange smell too, probably a combination of the raw meat and the sweat of the workers.

Doug's grandfather had owned and operated one of the stalls in the meat market there, and Doug often went in on Saturdays to help with the family business. I wonder if Doug was there on a Saturday helping his grandpa when my dad and I were there. Maybe we shopped at his grandfather's market; who knows? Could we have been within a few feet of each other as children, and then met thirty years later? Thinking of that gives me chills.

Do what you can where you are with what you have.

—Theodore Roosevelt, twenty-sixth
president of the United States

I was not prepared for Jed's release from prison in 2007, two years after he went in and a year after I met Doug. In my darkest moments, I fantasized that he would be a victim in prison, and never come out and try to get back into my boys' lives. But it turned out that he was in a "special unit" with other men who had been convicted of similar crimes and well-protected from the general prison population.

When he got out, he wanted to see the kids, and I wanted those visits to be supervised by another adult. I didn't want my kids to be alone with their father, but I also did not think I could be the one to oversee the visits. My boys were in the same age range as Jed's online targets. I wanted them to be safe, and I didn't trust Jed.

I went to court because he opposed the supervision. Probate court is always a gut-wrenching experience for anyone whose name appears on the docket. Unless you are there for an adoption, you are not there for a happy reason, and it's quite likely that the issue that brings you there is the cause of heartache in your life. You are divorcing or you are fighting over money and assets in your divorce. You can pick out the participants involved in a divorce by their anger or their tears. I was sweating as I waited for our case to be called, I had a knot in my stomach, and I was shaking all over.

When the clerk called our names, I moved up to respond to the judge's questions, and I noticed out of the corner of my eye that the court officer was moving toward me. I wasn't sure why, at first, but then I saw the officer staring down toward Jed's lower leg. He had seen the electronic ankle monitor that Jed wore as a condition of his release from prison. The officer must have thought that I might need protection. I was touched by the officer's taking a few steps toward me in that busy, crowded courtroom. It was a huge relief to see that someone else understood, and I felt vindicated somehow.

In the end, the judge ordered that a guardian ad litem (GAL) be appointed.

A GAL is an independent third party appointed by the court to investigate a situation and ascertain what will be "in the best interest of the child." The judge appointed an attorney from Cambridge, and I felt like I had lost this round in court. I didn't understand why the judge felt the need to investigate. Jed had been arrested for attempting to solicit a minor male. My sons were minor males. What was there to investigate? Someone needed to supervise the visits. I was shocked that there was even any discussion about this.

After the GAL was appointed, the process was upsetting for both the kids and me. We were all interviewed at agreed-upon times, and she came to our house for the meetings. These sessions were challenging for the three of us because of the difficult questions that she asked: Did the boys want to see their dad? Were they fearful of their dad? What did the boys understand about the criminal case?

The kids' counselor was interviewed as well. He told me later that he had to show her his notes from all our office visits, and her comment after reading them was something along the lines of, "It seems like these counseling sessions were difficult, how sad." I thought, *No shit, Sherlock!*

In the end, supervision was ordered.

Next came the challenge of who would supervise. Jed had prepared a list of people that he thought would be appropriate. It was silly how far off he was. His list consisted mostly of the parents of our boys' playmates, kids who had played with our kids two and three years ago when he lived with us. These people were not really our friends, and I didn't feel comfortable asking them to take on the difficult task of supervising visits.

When I asked the Guidance Department in our school for advice, they gave me the name of an agency that could provide a supervisor. We tried this route, but it didn't work well. I contacted the agency and was assigned a woman, and we had a lengthy phone conversation in which I had to tell her why we needed her to supervise. She was expensive, and her presence made the kids uncomfortable. She sat and took notes, and the kids felt as if they had done something wrong. Jed didn't appreciate her steely gaze on him. I didn't care that he didn't like the arrangement, but I didn't like her costs, and I wanted the kids to be comfortable. At this point in time, both kids would sometimes opt out of visits with their dad.

Once again, our good friends came to the rescue. After endless rounds back and forth with his list, and after approaching two people who said no, we were both able to agree on our neighbor Maria and my best friend, Luisa, and her husband. Both women had been in the trenches with us right from the start, and I was grateful for their willingness to step back into the middle of our mess with us. Jed's idea was to have Bobby help out in his store, ringing up sales and counting the money. Bobby was excited to help, and Michael did not want to go on this particular day. I drove Maria and Bobby and dropped them off at his café. An hour later, when I picked them up, I could tell that she was angry, but she didn't talk about it until later when she called me, because she didn't want Bobby to hear her. "Jed doesn't get it," she said. "He acts like this is no big deal, so nonchalant."

I told her that she didn't have to do any more visits; it was just too difficult. She was upset and I felt that I couldn't ask her to keep supervising if it was going to cause her grief. She had done so much for us already.

Over the next two years, Luisa and her husband, Mike, did all the supervising. They were unflappable, always calm, and their presence made me feel confident about my kids' safety. As supervisors, they stayed near the boys at all times so Jed couldn't say or do anything that was inappropriate or dangerous. No matter how many times he told me that he wouldn't harm our kids, I needed a supervisor because I didn't trust him. My kids felt comfortable with them, and they were extraordinarily generous with their time, even driving the boys so I had less interaction with Jed. The boys liked having their "aunt and uncle" accompany them. It felt more relaxed and less formal than the visits with the paid supervisor.

In the years after the arrest, I often got frustrated with Jed. It didn't seem to matter how many times I said that he needed to ask me first, he would talk to the kids and ask them if they wanted to do something on a certain day. Inevitably, they would get excited about whatever plan he had made, and I had to be the one to break the news that they couldn't go because they had CCD, or a dentist appointment, or whatever. Dealing with Jed was like dealing with a small child. He just didn't "get" so many things.

Once the boys got their driver's licenses, they began to make their own plans with their father. They would tell me the plan, and we would write it on the big calendar in the kitchen. Usually they got a bite to eat. I was always surprised—and relieved—at how short the visits were.

It was scary and yet a wonderful relief when the boys drove themselves to visit with their dad. I was so relieved that they had each other—they usually wouldn't say much to me about how the visit went. They were older and told me less, I guess because they were teenagers. I was comforted knowing that on the way and on the way back, alone in the car, they could vent to each other about their dad.

In Massachusetts you have to be sixteen and a half to get a driver's license. Like most teenagers, long before Michael turned sixteen, he was looking forward to getting his license. I didn't have the money to buy another car for him to use, so he knew that he had to earn and save his money to be able to buy his own car. During the summer that he turned sixteen, Michael worked full time at the day camp that he and Bobby had attended and loved. He also worked nights and weekends at the local grocery store and saved most of his earnings from both jobs. Doug admired Michael's two-job effort that summer and offered to help him in his quest for a car. He often went to vehicle auctions, and because of his mechanical ability, he could look under the hood and find great deals. The auctions offer much better prices than a used car dealer, but you have to know what you're buying.

Doug was a frequent flyer at many vehicle auctions, often buying equipment for his business.

After Doug and Michael discussed Michael's budget, Doug went to an auction on a hot summer day. He told me that he wanted to find a small truck for my boy, something solid that would protect a new driver. Michael might have had dreams of a Camaro or a similar hot rod, but he didn't make any specific request. I think he trusted Doug to get him something reliable and affordable. Before noon Doug called me to report that he had landed a small truck for Michael. The morning after the auction was a Saturday; Doug and Michael set off for the auction to pick up the truck and load it on one of Doug's trailers to bring it home. Doug's kids, Bobby, and I all were anxiously awaiting the arrival of the new truck. It was very exciting when we saw them round the corner and pull into the yard, Doug beeping the horn and Michael waving from the passenger seat. The new truck was white and it sat up high on the trailer—we could see it as soon as they pulled in, and we began to cheer and clap. We surrounded the trailer and climbed up to inspect Michael's new truck as soon as Doug stopped. My son was grinning from ear to ear and was so proud to show us his Dakota. He flashed the lights, turned on the wipers, and blasted the radio for us. The other four kids were in awe, and Bobby asked me, "Mom, can I start saving so I can buy a truck when I get my license?"

"Yes, work hard and save your money!" I said. What a great example Michael set for his brother and soon-to-be stepsiblings. He often looked back on that summer later. He was proud of how hard he worked and how much he had saved. Doug had found Michael a great deal; at a used car lot, the truck would have been out of a kid's price range. Doug's willingness to help us with this meant the world to me. He took on the task of finding a vehicle, did a fantastic job with it, and all I had to do was celebrate. It was his first time being a stepdad to my son, and when we became engaged a short while later,

I was confident that Doug would be there for my kids too, and not just for me.

Michael drove that truck for six years and sold it after he graduated from college. It started up every day and provided dependable transportation. A few years later, when Bobby turned sixteen, Doug went to an auction and once again found a great truck within a teen's budget.

Joy does not simply happen to us. We have to choose joy and keep choosing it every day.

—Henri Nouwen

After dating for two years, Doug and I decided it was time to think about making things permanent. We were crazy about each other and always felt like we didn't have enough time together. We lived forty minutes apart, and with our busy work schedules, plus our kids' activities, we didn't see each other as much as we wanted to. When we did get everyone together, we always had fun. The seven of us had spent time together at the kids' sporting events, on Doug's boat, skiing, or just having dinner at one house or the other. Over the course of the two years that we dated, we had all connected and begun to form real bonds. I will never forget one Mother's Day when Doug's girls made me a huge brunch, which we all enjoyed.

We had both been badly burned in our first marriages, and if we hadn't had young kids, we might have just moved in together and skipped the formalities. But with four teens and a tween, we felt we should set a good example; we needed to make a commitment, and living together just didn't feel right.

He proposed on a beautiful fall day while we were out on his boat.

Immediately, my planner brain went into overdrive. I wanted to be with him right away, but there were so many logistical issues. We each owned a house, at least one of which would need to be sold so we could buy a new one. Neither house would fit all of us, and we also needed something midway between where we lived now to make commuting to work and school more feasible. It also seemed more equitable to our many kids if we all started fresh in a new place, instead of trying to fit everyone into a house that some of us had already lived in.

There was a part of me that wanted a huge, catered, fancy party to celebrate our new marriage, but that would have been a foolish choice financially. In addition, Doug was shy, and the thought of a big wedding made him twitch. We decided on a small wedding day celebration, followed by a party at our new house once we settled in there. At first, we thought we would put both houses on the market, sell one, look for a new house, and then get married.

The problem with that scenario was in not knowing when a house might sell. If we did things in that order, I would have no time to plan the wedding. It also would be very hectic to sell a house, search for a new one, and plan the wedding simultaneously.

After mulling everything over for couple of months, we decided that we should plan the wedding and enjoy that, even if it meant having a commuter marriage afterward. We put the houses on the market in January, and we got married in Vermont during our February school vacation week, in a blizzard! We got married at the beginning of vacation so the seven of us could ski and hang out all week—a sort of honeymoon for seven! We had just a couple of friends and our parents at the wedding, and it was perfect.

The day after the wedding, while we were skiing, the real estate broker called me to say that we'd had an offer on my house, and I had chills. I was on the bunny slope and called Doug, who was on the chairlift. "Sweetie, you won't believe it—we have an offer on my house! The buyers are preapproved." I was jumping around as I told him.

"We'd better start looking for a house to buy," he said. We were both elated. Someone was watching over us. I knew that we had done the right thing, and incredibly—finally—things seemed to be falling into place for us.

As soon as we got back from our wedding week, we started looking at real estate listings, and we found a great house across the street from a lake. For two months, we commuted, and then in April, we sold my house and bought the new one on the same day. Ironically, moving day was twenty years, almost to the day, since my first wedding. I felt a strange mix of sadness, happiness, and relief to be moving from the house where I had lived as a young bride and when my babies were born. We rented Doug's house for several years and then sold it. My mom stayed in town and moved into senior housing.

When Doug and I got married, we had between us a junior in high school, a sophomore in high school, two eighth graders, and a sixth grader. My kids were with us all the time because I had full custody, and his went back and forth between their mom's house and ours. In the end, our five children graduated from five differ-ent high schools—and as a result, they knew every kid their age in a fifteen-mile radius, and everyone knew them. Michael finished his junior and senior year in the town he had grown up in, driving back and forth from our new house. Bobby decided to go to school in the new town, and we knew we had chosen well once he made that announcement. He could have stayed where he had grown up, since I was still teaching there. Our new home was in Hopkinton. We loved the house and knew the schools were fantastic.

Doug's oldest chose a public high school with a pool and a great swim program. She was able to go there due to the "school choice" program. My stepson went to a private school for hockey, and my younger stepdaughter eventually went to the public school in the town where her mom's house was located. Five kids, five high schools!

Somehow, we made it work. Community and family are more powerful than everything else. Doug teased me sometimes when we first moved in together. "Nice community you built," he'd say while the kids were watching TV together, or laughing at the dinner table. Each of the angels who helped us after the arrest played a part in bringing us through the difficult times, to this new family.

Common conversation at our dinner table went like this: "Bobby, do you know a kid named John on your hockey team? I met him at lacrosse practice and he said he knows you."

Our two oldest went on a mission trip through church together and took the Red Cross lifeguard class together. Our eighth graders both played lots of sports and knew many of the same kids from teams.

Michael's graduation from high school was fourteen months after we moved into our new house. We wanted to throw him a party, and having people over was a great motivator to make some improvements on the house. Doug and I really wanted to work on the yard, and the sellers had left us with some half-done projects. A month before graduation, we began tackling our "to do" list. First was new back steps leading out to a patio. We hired a company to do that. Next, we decided that we needed some new shrubs in two places in the yard, and this seemed like a project that we could do ourselves.

We told all five of our kids that we needed them home on a Saturday in May to help plant some "bushes." They weren't pleased, but they all appeared at the designated time. When a huge tractor-trailer pulled into the driveway that morning, I was sure that the driver had the wrong house. He was hauling out ten six-foot arborvitaes. I'd thought we were putting in little bushes! These trees were so big that we would not be able to plant them in hand-dug holes. Next into the yard came the excavator that Doug would use to dig the holes. My husband had big plans for the yard and his untrained "staff" of landscapers.

Doug quickly became impatient with his crew, five crabby teenagers and his enthusiastic but not-very-handy wife—all of us totally inexperienced in this type of project. By the time the third hole was being dug, the kids had begun to lean on their shovels and whine about lunch. They looked like an underpaid group of laborers, counting the days until retirement. I think one or two tried to plead pressing homework assignments as an exit strategy. We held firm, though, and insisted that they keep helping. As Doug was taking the last tree off the truck with the excavator, all five kids had dropped their tools and were sitting on the lawn, waiting to be dismissed from the job. They were done.

I raced over to try and guide the tree off the truck. I had watched the process all day and figured, how hard could it be? The next thing I knew, the tree was swinging toward me, and I couldn't get out of the way of its momentum. It knocked me over, and I landed smack in the middle of the driveway on my butt. I wasn't hurt, but I was so angry!

I was mad at the kids for being less than enthusiastic and helpful. I was really mad at Doug who had bought giant trees and then lost patience with his inexperienced crew! I was exhausted from being Switzerland, the peace-keeping force between the grouchy teenagers and the foreman-boss-husband. I yelled to him, "You know, none of us have ever planted big trees before. None of us know what we're doing except for you!"

His response was, "Go big or go home." Then we both began to crack up and dissolved into laughter. It was a crazy, ridiculous day that we have laughed about often since then.

By the day of the party, we were all telling the story to the guests as they raved about our beautiful new trees.

Just before Michael started his freshman year in college, he received an email informing him that he would be in a "triple." All the dorm rooms in his building were designed to be doubles, but due to high enrollment numbers, his room and a few others would be triples. My son was upset and thought that I should ask for a partial refund for the cost of the housing. I told him the story about my parents and my sophomore-year dorm. I went on to tell him how thrilled I was that he was going to an amazing university and that I was sure it would all work out well. One of his roommates left by Halloween that year, then another freshman moved in from down the hall to take the place of the kid who had left. The new group of three guys lived together all four years, and I believe that they will be lifelong friends. No complaints about dorm rooms from this mom—my parents had taught me well.

*Our hearts grow tender with childhood memories and love of
kindred, and we are better throughout the year for having,
in spirit, become a child again at Christmastime.*

—Laura Ingalls Wilder, American educator and author

These days, Christmas is very busy for this Santa. There are two sons,
one stepson, two stepdaughters, and a husband to shop for now.
Michael is busy working as an attorney. We are delighted that he is
able to take time off and come home to celebrate with us. Bobby is
getting ready to head to Georgia in February to start his Army OCS
training. There were three graduations last May: Bobby and Doug's
son from college and Michael from law school, so lots of parental joy
that weekend.

My stepson has a great job which uses his economics degree. He
still lives nearby so we get to see him often; once in a while he skates
with his dad in Doug's "old man" hockey league. Doug is so proud of
him and enjoys hockey most when his son is there.

The youngest needs luggage this Christmas as she gets ready for
her semester abroad. We are hoping to visit her while she is away

studying, as we are both busy with work and looking forward to a vacation. His oldest just started a new job, and we will all be eager to hear the details. In a few years, our kids may have moved, or maybe they will be married and will celebrate Christmas at their in-laws' house. This year, though, we are thrilled that they are all here with us.

In the weeks leading up to Christmas, Doug and I take turns having moments that stop us in our tracks remembering the years after we divorced our first spouses and before we met; years when Christmases were sad and difficult. Being broke, lonely, and having to schedule the kids' holiday visit with the ex was anything but festive and joyful. We are happy together in our home now and grateful that we are together. Having a partner, a teammate, and a loving companion is one of life's greatest gifts and something we will never take for granted.

While Michael is home, he and Doug will be up early in the morning discussing current events and the state of the stock market. I love hearing them solve all the world's problems while I putter in the kitchen. Michael's Christmas present to Bobby was tickets for the two of them for the Celtics game on December 23; they always schedule some "brother time" when they are both home, and my heart is glad of that.

The kids are so helpful now. "What can I do?" is frequently heard from these now-adults who haul out the trash, empty the dishwasher, make the last-minute trip to the grocery store, help me put away the leftovers, and drive their elderly relatives without complaint. These five are a joy to be around.

Doug enjoys cooking, so I will trek to the coast to buy fresh fish, and he will create a feast for Christmas Eve. Our neighbors will relish the smells coming from the deep fryer when the turkey goes into the pot on the patio on Christmas day. When I look around the table, I close my eyes, and I can picture the kids when Doug and I met: they ranged in age from nine to fourteen then. They were so young! All in their twenties now, we have come a long way on our journey to creating a family. The dining room table is our gathering spot, and there is always a lot of laughter when the seven of us are together. They now share stories about college and work rather than the sports that they were all busy with as teenagers.

Doug's dad has passed, and his mother is suffering in a nursing home with Alzheimer's. My mom is frail but still loves to dress up and come to our house to see her grandsons and her step-grandchildren. She still looks for every opportunity to bake for someone who is sick or to volunteer at church.

Doug's parents and my mom were so happy when we got married. His dad told us that we were a good team, and his approval meant a lot. Each set of grandparents bought gifts for all five kids at Christmas, and we loved their inclusive thoughtfulness.

This year we volunteered at several events to raise money for the National Multiple Sclerosis Society. I am touched when my family comes with me to work and support my cause. Muckfest has been a highlight: I don't race the course, I have to walk, and I skip some of the obstacles. But being there, crawling in the mud, and having Bobby yell, "Come on, Mom, you can do it" makes for a fantastic day. Muckfest has become one of my favorite fundraising events, but we have also walked for MS, and helped at a regatta and a golf tournament.

We all love Christmastime: the tree, the lights, the music, the cookies, and being together at home. I am touched when the boys tell me about what they bought for Toys for Tots, what community service project they did, or what organization they donated to. I am glad that my parents' legacy of service made its way to them. We had so much help when things went wrong in our family that I'm not certain I will ever be able to pay it all forward.

Jed isn't really part of the boys' lives. He wasn't invited to confirmations or graduations. Bobby hasn't spoken to him for several years; there is too much hurt and upset. Michael meets him for breakfast or lunch when he is back in Massachusetts visiting us. Jed continued living with his mom until the sentencing. When he was released from jail, he convinced her to buy a multifamily house so he could live in one apartment and she could rent out the rest. One day I sat down and added up what his mother had spent on his legal defense, business, and housing. My conservative estimate was that his ride to New Hampshire to meet the police officer cost her half a million dollars, perhaps even more. However he got the money, Jed always paid the child support, thankfully.

After eleven years in special education, I left the teaching world to help Doug run his business. The flexibility of my working with him gives us more freedom to take off and have fun; I can tag along when he looks at a job on a random Tuesday. We often stay over and make a mini-vacation out of the work trip. My new, less rigid work schedule also gives me extra time to take care of our aging moms.

In addition to working with Doug, I have a small real estate practice, and I love using my legal skills again.

Bobby's godfather, Jon, and his wife and three sons live in our town now. He and I chat often about his little boys, my big boys, and his busy family; he is truly the brother that I never had. I am honored when he asks my opinion about a parenting issue. He says he learned a lot from me, and I am humbled by that. He has been a dedicated uncle to my sons, and we love being a part of his boys' lives, going to their sporting events whenever we can.

In between wrapping and baking, I need to see my neurologist for my annual checkup and MRIs. To this day, despite having at least one MRI a year, and more if I have an MS-related issue, I am happy to say that I can tolerate them and I have never seen the inside of the tube thanks to that first tech offering me a facecloth. I have several friends who admit that they can't tolerate the closed space; they were told to keep their eyes closed and they peeked! I always think of the first MRI with Trish, even now.

I still hate to go to the hospital, even as an outpatient, but I am so grateful for the excellent care my neurologist has provided. The fatigue is the toughest part of MS for me, and it's especially hard to stay well rested at Christmastime. I want to stay up late and visit with everyone, and I don't like missing out on anything fun. I feel very fortunate that I have no ongoing mobility issues with the MS. I am lucky to battle only the fatigue, compared with many other patients with greater struggles. I still inject the MS medicine, and I vividly remember how terrified I was when I first learned that I would have to give myself shots. I still don't love doing it, but the process is routine now. Thankfully the medicine continues to work for me.

Linda has an annual Christmas party, which Doug and I look forward to each year. It gives me a chance to see many old friends in person. I still talk to Luisa and Trish nearly every week with visits to catch up in person whenever we can arrange them. Maria is still "Aunt Maria" to my boys, and she will always have a special place in their hearts.

My cousin Jim and his wife will come to our house for Christmas Eve, and they are so much fun to be with. We always love it when we get to spend time with them. Our divorces became final at around the same time, and, coincidentally, we married again in the same year. We are both happy now, and when we look back, we can't quite believe what we've been through. It has been a blessing to have someone who understands all the baggage that comes with your spouse walking out and leaving you and your kids. How odd that in such a small family two cousins had a similarly gut-wrenching experience.

Our family dentist is still the same wonderful Dr. Ted, and because of him, we look forward to dental appointments in a way that most people don't. Now he hugs me when I see him, we both get teary, and he asks how my "men" are doing. He speaks volumes without saying much. I always say, "Remember when you came to two baseball games?" And he shrugs it off as if to say, "No big deal."

Last summer when both boys were home, we invited Nick to dinner. It had been ages since we'd seen him in person, although social media has kept him in touch with Michael and Bobby. We laughed all through the meal, reminiscing about the many events Nick came to in support of my kids. He works with children now in his career and says we were his "first" family. Any family he works with will benefit from his insight, his kindness, and his enthusiasm for life.

I always have at least one vase full of holly in the house at this time of year. We have a gorgeous holly bush in our yard, and having those sprigs inside the house reminds me of my dad. I think he would be pleased with what I have accomplished in my life. I know he would be proud of my sons and the men that they have become.

Epilogue

April 2018

Twenty-three days after I submitted the first few pages of this book to She Writes Press, hoping to receive a contract for publication, Doug passed away suddenly. We had planned to go skiing for a few days in Vermont, his favorite place, later that day.

I am still trying to wrap my head around this stunning loss. There are no words. His wake and memorial service were attended by hundreds of people. Doug touched many lives with his warmth and his loyalty. I feel that we have been robbed for having had him such a short time, but I am certain of his love, and I hope that will sustain me. I will always remember Doug's enthusiasm for a beautiful sunset, a steep trail with fresh powder, a good joke, a giant striper, a game of pond hockey, a cold beer at the end of a busy day, or a momma deer and her babies on the side of a road.

We were married nine years, one month, one week, and a few days. His legacy of working hard and playing hard will carry on in us as the kids and I try to live each day as he would have, always choosing to "Go big, or go home." Doug and I showed each other that true love was still possible, even after experiencing great hardship and broken hearts. He was the love of my life.

Acknowledgments

Thank you Mom for always believing in me and teaching me strength.

To my W. Roxbury friends, thank you for many years of support and friendship.

To my terrific stepchildren—you are the bonus that came when I fell in love with your dad.

Beth, Linda, Luisa, Marylee, Maria, Patty, and Trish—what an amazing army of thoughtful, caring women we had holding us up. Without you, I don't know what we would have done. Thank you.

John and Jon, true gentlemen in every sense of the word and warriors for my boys. I will always be grateful.

Jimmy, the best cousin.

Stu for telling me that I should teach so I could take care of my boys—it seemed like a crazy idea at first, but it made all the difference in our lives. Thank you.

To the community who rallied around us and cared for us, thank you.

Ruth, principal of our middle school—for watching over my

boys, hiring me to teach, and protecting the three of us while we were in your school. Thank you.

Maryann, Rose, and the rest of the Wilson staff for holding me up every day and for taking care of the boys. Thank you.

Edith, for helping me figure out how to become a stepmother. Thank you for sharing the journey with me.

Maria for teaching me how to handle a chronic illness: take the medicine, listen to the doctors, always apply makeup before leaving the house, then do your best to forget about the illness and live your life. Thank you.

Marybeth, the best neurologist, for providing me with excellent care and always being available. Thank you.

Nick, you were so young but so wise. You came into our family when we needed you and you became an important part of our lives. Thank you.

Nadine Kenney Johnstone, the best writing coach—you helped a novice feel like a pro. Thank you for your enthusiasm for my project and your endless encouragement when I ran into writing roadblocks. Without your wisdom and your guidance, this book would still be just a dream of mine.

About the Author

© Chris Loomis

Following a fifteen-year career as an attorney, Diane Stelfox Cook became a special education teacher, serving in the Massachusetts public schools for eleven years. Today, she runs her late husband's construction company. A native of Boston, Cook attended Boston Latin School, the nation's oldest public school, and holds a bachelor's degree from Clark University, a master's degree in education from Framingham State University, and a law degree from Suffolk University Law School. She is a voracious reader who is always looking for a new legal thriller, a lover of all things aquatic, including kayaking and swimming, and a diehard fan of her sons' alma mater football teams, Notre Dame's Fighting Irish and Virginia Tech's Hokies. She continues to practice law part time.

SELECTED TITLES FROM SHE WRITES PRESS

She Writes Press is an independent publishing company founded to serve women writers everywhere. Visit us at www.shewritespress.com.

The Buddha at My Table: How I Found Peace in Betrayal and Divorce by Tammy Letherer $16.95, 978-1-63152-425-7
On a Tuesday night, just before Christmas, after he had put their three children in bed, Tammy Letherer's husband shattered her world and destroyed every assumption she'd ever made about love, friendship, and faithfulness. In the aftermath of this betrayal, however, she finds unexpected blessings—and, ultimately, the path to freedom.

Filling Her Shoes: Memoir of an Inherited Family by Betsy Graziani Fasbinder $16.95, 978-1-63152-198-0. A "sweet-bitter" story of how, with tenderness as their guide, a family formed in the wake of loss and learned that joy and grief can be entwined cohabitants in our lives.

Pieces of Me: Rescuing My Kidnapped Daughters by Lizbeth Meredith !16.95 978-1-63152-834-7
When her daughters are kidnapped and taken to Greece by their non-custodial father, single mom Lizbeth Meredith vows to bring them home—and give them a better childhood than her own.

Hug Everyone You Know: A Year of Community, Courage, and Cancer by Antoinette Truglio Martin $16.95, 978-1-63152-262-8
Cancer is scary enough for the brave, but for a wimp like Antoinette Martin, it was downright terrifying. With the help of her community, however, Martin slowly found the courage within herself to face cancer—and to do so with perseverance and humor.

Renewable: One Woman's Search for Simplicity, Faithfulness, and Hope by Eileen Flanagan $16.95, 978-1-63152-968-9
At age forty-nine, Eileen Flanagan had an aching feeling that she wasn't living up to her youthful ideals or potential, so she started trying to change the world—and in doing so, she found the courage to change her life.

Printed in the United States
by Baker & Taylor Publisher Services